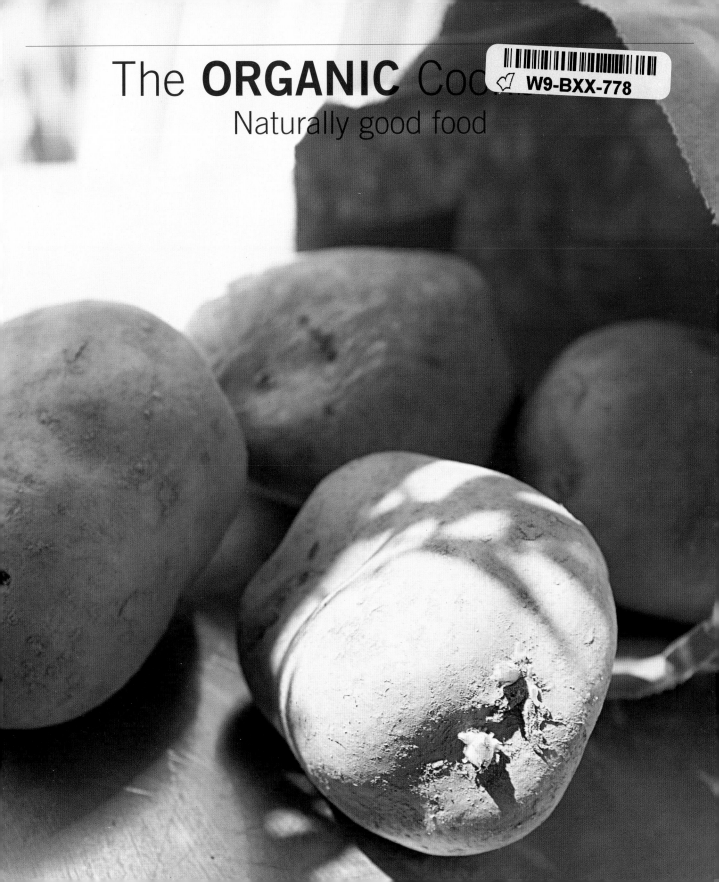

# The **ORGANIC** Coo...

## Naturally good food

# The **ORGANIC** Cookbook

### Renée J Elliott & Eric Treuillé

Photography by Ian O'Leary

A Dorling Kindersley Book

Dorling  Kindersley

LONDON, NEW YORK, SYDNEY,
DELHI, PARIS, MUNICH, and
JOHANNESBURG

**DEDICATIONS**
FROM RENÉE ELLIOTT
To Mom

FROM ERIC TREUILLÉ
This book is dedicated to:
Everyone at Sheepdrove Organic Farm,
but especially Charles Maclean and
Peter Kindersley, for giving me a chance
to participate in a commerical organic
farm in action. Also to Anabel and
Juliet Kindersley, two busy mothers
who garden, shop, cook and eat
organic – these recipes are for you.
And lastly to Eliette Gardou. I grew up
in an intensely rural part of the South
West of France, among people deeply
connected to their land and the natural
rhythms of this earth. Most are gone,
but Eliette is still at Le Turelet and
remains my teacher and my inspiration.

First American edition, 2001
01 02 03 04 05 10 9 8 7 6 5 4 3 2 1

Published in the United States by
Dorling Kindersley Publishing, Inc.
95 Madison Avenue
New York, NY 10016

A Cataloging-in-Publication record is
available from the Library of Congress

ISBN 0-7894-7192-2

Reproduced in Italy by GRB
Editrice,Verona
Printed in Italy by Printer Trento S.r.l.

Organic Cookbook is meant to be used as a
general recipe book and source of information,
not a medical reference book. While every
effort has been made to ensure that the
contents of this book are accurate, it is not
intended to be prescriptive and should in no
way be treated as a substitute or alternative to
qualified medical advice.

See our complete catalog at
**www.dk.com**

# Contents

# Choose Organic

Chefs and food lovers the world over all agree that to cook good food, you have to start with good ingredients.

**GOOD FOR YOU** Organic food is good for us, good for our planet and good to eat. Organic cooking begins with organic ingredients, but goes beyond the contents of your shopping basket. To cook organic is more than a buying decision. It is a lifestyle choice, and an attitude that informs the way we cook, eat and shop.

**FLAVOR WITHOUT FUSS** The organic way to cook is about making every ingredient count. The aim is to enhance, not disguise. The better the quality of the ingredients, the less you need to do to them. When you switch to organic ingredients, the much quoted maxim, "keep it simple" is more relevant than ever. For today's time-challenged cooks, this is good news. Cooking organic means flavor without fuss.

**THE SIMPLER THE BETTER** Cooking organic is based on selecting good ingredients and handling them minimally in a way that their distinctive flavor, texture and aroma can be best appreciated. The ingredients are the star and the recipe is their showcase. The simpler, the better. Our recipe selection is intended to reflect this – dishes based on classic combinations and straight-forward cooking techniques. Forget time-consuming recipes and multiple "fusion" flavors. Let the ingredients speak for themselves.

## THE NATURAL CHOICE

Organic farming is a carefully defined system of food production, strictly monitored and enforced by law to meet rigorous standards. Organic farmers seek to work with nature rather than control it with chemicals. Organic principles are underpinned by the following:

- *Soil fertility*
- *Free from artificial chemical fertilisers*
- *Free from pesticides*
- *Free from Genetically Modified Organisms*
- *Minimal damage to the environment*
- *Minimal processing and additives*

It is ironic that we refer to the use of chemicals in agriculture as "conventional". Contrary to popular perception, its practice is a wholly new experiment in the history of food production. It is a mere blip in time over the thousands of years since farming began. In reality, it is organic farming, with its combination of modern soil science and traditional, tried-and-tested methods, that is truly the agriculture of today and tomorrow. A sustainable farming system that is free from artificial chemicals produces high-quality food and protects the environment. It is our best option for a future if we are to conserve the earth's precious and finite resources.

## RECIPES TO INSPIRE

At every opportunity, we have made our recipes open to adaptation. Often we give a basic recipe with variations that substitute different ingredients but use identical techniques. Alternatively, a recipe is given with a list of the possible ingredients that can be adjusted according to personal preference or availability of ingredients. We suggest alternative ingredients and optional additions to allow the cook to vary a dish according to the season, occasion, mood or simply to what's in the cupboard. Recipes are but points of departure. Cooking is a flexible, responsive process; the time, the place and the person all play a role in its special alchemy.

## BUYING ORGANIC, BUYING WHAT'S BEST

This process starts with the shopping basket. The organic cook is an opportunistic shopper who buys what's best on the day. Shop with all your senses. Look, smell, touch, and taste too, if you can, before you buy. Organic ingredients may not be entirely uniform or cosmetically perfect, but, when freshly harvested in their natural season, they have a sheen, a perfume and a vitality that artificially cultivated produce rarely has. Ingredients differ from season to season and day to day, so once in the kitchen, remember to taste before and while you cook.

## BE CREATIVE

Remain open to variation and don't be afraid to change seasoning to suit your palate. Cooking is creative, rewarding and fun. Every day, you get to be an artist, inspired by color, texture, form and aroma, challenged by the blank canvas of a dinner plate. Make cooking pleasurable as well as pleasure-giving.

### GROUND RULES

The secret is in the soil. Intensive farming exhausts the soil, depleting the natural minerals and trace elements essential for nutrient-rich food. For the organic farmer, the soil and its natural fertility are paramount. Various non-artificial methods, such as mixed farming systems that integrate a range of crops with rearing livestock and crop rotation, are used to keep the soil in good health and replace essential nutrients. Appropriate varieties, beneficial predatory insects and companion planting help build resistance to pests and diseases. Naturally strong crops grown in fertile soil will take up a richer nutrient supply. Organic farming delivers healthy soil growing healthy plants producing healthy food.

**NATURALLY GOOD TASTE**

Organic food is produced as nature intended. Crops and livestock are grown and reared naturally, at their own pace, without artificial fertilisers, synthetic pesticides, chemical feeds, growth-promoting drugs or routine antibiotics. Because organic produce is allowed to develop more slowly, it generally contains less water and more solid matter, which means more nutrients and more flavor. In addition, organic farmers generally favor traditional varieties over modern hybrids and cross-breeds in order to promote biodiversity and to suit climatic conditions. Produce must be harvested at peak condition and transferred from field to store to cooking pot with minimal delay to maintain optimum nutrition and flavor. Industrial food processing and packaging methods can keep produce looking fresh for weeks or even months. Organic crops are not sprayed with post-harvest chemicals to prolong shelf life. Appearances do not deceive, as they do in non-organic produce. Truly fresh food will look, feel, smell and taste fresh.

TASTE AND GOODNESS Home cooked food may require more effort than picking up the phone to order take out or putting a frozen dinner in the microwave, but the results just don't compare in terms of taste, goodness or enjoyment. Everyone agrees that you are what you eat. Food is our life's sustenance and our first line of defense against disease. When you do the cooking, you're in control. You can ensure optimum nutrition and limit your exposure to the chemicals that non-organic farming practices and food processing methods involve.

RELAX AND NURTURE As the pace of modern life accelerates ever faster, cooking can be an immensely rewarding and relaxing routine at the end of a challenging day. There are few simple, everyday tasks more satisfying than preparing food for family and friends. The ritual of sitting down together to share a daily meal immeasurably enhances our quality of life. To feed is to nurture and to care for food is to care for ourselves. Eating together is an inclusive experience that nourishes both body and soul. Make time to enjoy it.

Shop with care, cook with pleasure, and eat slowly, in the company of those you love. Respect is at the heart of the organic revolution. Respect for our food, respect for ourselves, and respect for our land - land we hold in trust for future generations.

# Choose Seasonal

In the last 30 years, shopping for food has changed dramatically. Seasonal availability has become a thing of the past. We have grown used to having summer berries in winter and spring greens in fall. Today, almost any kind of food is available all year round and often at very low prices. But there are hidden costs.

# OUT OF SEASON, OUT OF FLAVOR

Buying food out of season means paying for food that has been picked unripe and transported thousands of miles under controlled atmosphere storage. High yield, cosmetic uniformity, long shelf life and the ability to withstand lengthy transportation are among the commercial criteria that dictate which fruit and vegetable varieties are grown. Taste and goodness are not. The longer the delay between field and plate, the greater the deterioration of flavor and nutrients.

When you buy ingredients in their natural season, they tend to be more plentiful, readily available, reasonably priced and at the peak of flavor and nutrition. A basic knowledge of what is in season is the first step towards top tasting, nutrient packed food.

# KNOWING WHEN IT'S BEST

The seasonal chart on page 10 is intended as a guide to when fresh produce is at its seasonal peak. We do not suggest that you never again buy the ingredients listed outside of these guidelines. Certain produce does store well and imported ingredients have always played an important role in our culinary traditions. Our aim is to encourage you to seize the opportunity of eating fresh food when it is at its peak and in plentiful supply.

# IN TUNE WITH THE SEASONS

It is time for us to renew our link with the rhythms of the natural world. Our bodies hunger for different foods at different times of year – hearty comfort food in the cold winter months, light, refreshing dishes in the summertime – and mother nature matches our moods and supplies our needs. Good produce, like great wine, should speak of the soil, the sun, the rain. The way it tastes will reflect its variety, as well as where it was grown, who grew it, and when it was harvested. Year round availability is limiting our choice and blunting our taste buds with consistently bland food. Shop, cook and eat in tune with the seasons, and the pleasure of eating vegetables and fruits at their appropriate time is yours.

## YOU ARE WHAT YOU EAT

Eating a healthy diet is one of the most important things we can do for ourselves. Our bodies are under stress from the fast pace of modern life, yet we live in an increasingly toxic environment, and the food we depend on to nourish and sustain us is treated with artificial chemicals, adulterated with artificial additives and depleted of essential nutrients. Our eating habits have changed drastically over the past twenty years. Food fads, yo-yo dieting and health scares have fostered fear of food and bred ignorance of healthy eating. If we want to eat well, feel good and live better, we need to put home cooked food made with the best ingredients back on the menu. Vote with your fork – choose organic.

## NATURAL SELECTION

The best way to shop for fresh seasonal produce is not to make a list at home, but to wait and see what looks and smells best at the market or store. To preserve maximum flavor and nutrition, store carefully (see pages 12-14) and eat as soon as you can.

# Seasonal guide

## Hearty Greens & Cabbages

| | SPRING | SUMMER | AUTUMN | WINTER |
|---|---|---|---|---|
| Spinach | ••• | ••• | ••• | • |
| Swiss Chard | ••• | | ••• | • |
| Collard Greens | ••• | | | •• |
| Kale | ••• | | | •• |
| Broccoli | | | | |
| *Calabrese* | •• | • | ••• | ••• |
| *Rabe* | ••• | | • | ••• |
| Cauliflower | •• | • | ••• | ••• |
| Cabbages | | | | |
| *Summer Green* | •• | •• | | |
| *Savoy* | •• | | ••• | •• |
| *Dutch* | •• | | •• | •• |
| *Red* | | • | ••• | •• |
| Brussel Sprouts | | | | •• |

## Shoots & Stalks

| | SPRING | SUMMER | AUTUMN | WINTER |
|---|---|---|---|---|
| Asparagus | ••• | | | |
| Globe Artichokes | | •• | • | |
| Fennel | •• | | ••• | ••• |
| Celery | ••• | ••• | ••• | ••• |

## Alliums & Onions

| | SPRING | SUMMER | AUTUMN | WINTER |
|---|---|---|---|---|
| Scallions | ••• | •• | | |
| Leeks | ••• | • | ••• | ••• |
| Garlic | | | | |
| *Green* | •• | • | | |
| *Dry* | | ••• | ••• | |
| Onions | • | | ••• | ••• |
| Shallots | | •• | ••• | ••• |

## Salads & Tender Greens

| | SPRING | SUMMER | AUTUMN | WINTER |
|---|---|---|---|---|
| Watercress | ••• | •• | •• | • |
| Sorrel | ••• | • | | |
| Arugula | ••• | | •• | • |
| Dandelion | •• | | | |
| Oakleaf | | •• | ••• | |
| Romaine | | •• | ••• | •• |
| Butterhead Lettuce | | • | ••• | |
| Escarole | ••• | • | ••• | •• |
| Frisee | ••• | | •• | •• |
| Radicchio | •• | | •• | •• |
| Belgian Endive | ••• | | ••• | ••• |
| Mizuna | ••• | | ••• | •• |

## Fresh Herbs

| | SPRING | SUMMER | AUTUMN | WINTER |
|---|---|---|---|---|
| Parsley | ••• | ••• | ••• | • |
| Chives | •• | ••• | ••• | |
| Mint | •• | ••• | •• | |
| Fennel | •• | ••• | ••• | |
| Marjoram | | ••• | ••• | |
| Oregano | | ••• | ••• | |
| Tarragon | | • | ••• | |
| Chervil | •• | | •• | |
| Dill | | •• | •• | |
| Basil | | ••• | • | |
| Thyme | ••• | ••• | ••• | ••• |
| Rosemary | ••• | ••• | ••• | ••• |
| Sage | ••• | ••• | ••• | ••• |
| Bay | ••• | ••• | ••• | ••• |

## Beans & Pods

| | SPRING | SUMMER | AUTUMN | WINTER |
|---|---|---|---|---|
| Fava beans | •• | •• | | |
| Garden Peas | • | •• | | |
| Haricots Verts | | ••• | • | |
| String Beans | | ••• | • | |
| Corn | | •• | • | |

## Squashes & Vegetable Fruits

| | SPRING | SUMMER | AUTUMN | WINTER |
|---|---|---|---|---|
| Avocados | ••• | ••• | ••• | ••• |
| Cucumbers | | ••• | • | |
| Summer Squashes | | ••• | • | |
| Zucchini | | ••• | • | |
| Tomatoes | | ••• | •• | |
| Okra | | ••• | •• | |
| Bell Peppers | | ••• | ••• | |
| Eggplant | | •• | •• | |
| Chiles | | • | | |
| Pumpkins | | | ••• | ••• |
| Winter Squashes | | | ••• | ••• |

## Roots & Tubers

| | Spring | Summer | Autumn | Winter |
|---|---|---|---|---|
| Radishes | | | | |
| Spring | • | • | | |
| Asian | | | • | • |
| Black | | | • | • |
| Turnips | | | | |
| Spring | | • | | |
| Storage | | | • | • |
| Carrots | | | | |
| Spring | • | • | | |
| Storage | | • | • | |
| Potatoes | | | | |
| New | | • | • | |
| Storage | • | | • | • |
| Sweet | • | | • | • |
| Beetroot | • | | • | • |
| Parsnips | • | • | • | • |
| Celery Root | • | | • | • |
| Salsify | • | | • | • |
| Rutabaga | • | | • | • |
| Jerusalem | | | • | • |
| Artichokes | • | | • | • |

## Wild Mushrooms & Fungi

| | Spring | Summer | Autumn | Winter |
|---|---|---|---|---|
| Morels | • | • | | |
| Chanterelles | | • | • | |
| Porcini | | • | • | |
| Field Mushrooms | | • | • | |
| Truffles | | | • | • |

## Orchard Fruits

| | Spring | Summer | Autumn | Winter |
|---|---|---|---|---|
| Cherries | | • | | |
| Apricots | | • | | |
| Peaches | | • | • | |
| Nectarines | | • | • | |
| Plums | | • | • | |
| Figs | | • | • | |
| Mulberries | | • | • | |
| Pears | | • | • | • |
| Apples | • | • | • | • |
| Quinces | | | • | |

## Citrus Fruits

| | Spring | Summer | Autumn | Winter |
|---|---|---|---|---|
| Lemons | • | • | • | • |
| Oranges | | | | |
| Sweet | • | • | • | • |
| Blood | • | | • | • |
| Sour | | | | • |
| Grapefruit | • | • | • | • |
| Mandarins | • | | • | • |
| Kumquats | • | | • | • |
| Limes | | • | • | • |
| Key Limes | • | • | • | • |
| Meyer Lemons | • | | • | • |

## Vegetable Fruits

| | Spring | Summer | Autumn | Winter |
|---|---|---|---|---|
| Rhubarb | | | | |
| Glasshouse | • | | | • |
| Field | • | • | | |
| Melons | | • | • | |
| Watermelons | | • | • | |

## Soft & Vine Fruits

| | Spring | Summer | Autumn | Winter |
|---|---|---|---|---|
| Strawberries | • | • | • | |
| Raspberries | | • | • | |
| Gooseberries | | • | | |
| Currants | | | | |
| Red & White | | • | | |
| Black | | • | | |
| Grapes | | • | • | |
| Blueberries | | • | • | |
| Blackberries | | • | • | |
| Elderberries | | | • | |
| Cranberries | | | • | • |

## Tropical Fruit

| | Spring | Summer | Autumn | Winter |
|---|---|---|---|---|
| Bananas | • | • | • | • |
| Pineapples | • | • | • | • |
| Papayas | • | • | • | • |
| Mangos | • | • | • | • |
| Passion Fruit | • | • | • | • |
| Pomegranates | | | • | • |
| Kiwis | • | | • | • |
| Dates | | | • | • |
| Persimmons | | | • | • |

# Shop Organic

**BEST BUYS**
For optimum, nutrient packed food, choose locally grown produce in its natural season, especially when there is no organic option on the shelves. When making your buying decisions, let the following criteria guide you to the healthiest choices:

## Buy organic
## Buy in season
## Buy local

**SPEAK UP!**
What you buy, what you ask for, and what you complain about all play a part in determining the quality and availability of fresh produce in your store. Be prepared to speak up! If they are not selling something, ask for it.

**GOODNESS INSIDE OUT**
A natural bristle brush is an essential piece of equipment in the organic kitchen. Use it to clean the skins of all fruits and vegetables.

When the peel or skin of fruit and vegetables is edible, leave unpeeled where you can, as the skin and the flesh just beneath the skin are rich in nutrients and fiber. If not organically grown, always peel thoroughly, as even washing with soap or detergent will not remove fungicide and pesticide residues on the skin.

Good cooking and healthy eating begin with careful shopping and proper storage. Refer to our seasonal chart to get an idea of the seasonal fresh produce you can expect to find in the store. Take time to examine fruit and vegetables before you buy, as their look, feel and smell will tell you a lot about their quality. Get your shopping home without delay, store appropriately and prepare as close to cooking as possible to preserve optimum nutrition. Taste and goodness diminish over time, so the sooner you eat fresh produce, the fuller its flavor and the higher its nutritive value.

Choose fruit and vegetables that look fresh, healthy and 'alive'. Organic produce may not be cosmetically perfect but should not be substandard. Minor blemishes or irregularities are fine, but bruises, soft spots and splits are not. Be prepared to hold, press and sniff as you shop. Fresh produce that is heavy for its size tends to be more succulent and flavorful, while the key to judging ripeness in many fruits and some vegetables is their aroma. A ripe tomato will smell of tomato in a way that a hydroponically-grown tomato never will. The best option for storing most vegetables and some fruits is in a loosely closed plastic bag with holes pricked in it placed in the vegetable crisper bin of the refrigerator. Always remove from their wrapping any fruit or vegetables that have been sold sealed in plastic or they will sweat and deteriorate.

Hearty greens should look lively and feel squeaky fresh. Any yellowing or limpness indicates age. Spinach is best bought loose, as pre-packed plastic bags often conceal bruised or wilted leaves. Store greens unwashed and refrigerated for up to 4 days.

Choose cabbages with compact heads that feel heavy for their size, and cauliflower or broccoli with tightly formed, crisp looking florets. Refrigerated, cabbages will keep for up to 1 month, cauliflower and broccoli for up to 5 days.

Check the cut ends of shoots such as artichokes and asparagus. If they are brown and dry, they were harvested some time ago. The leaves on artichoke heads and the scales on asparagus tips should be tightly closed like new flower buds, which is essentially what they are. Like flowers, they are best stored with their stems immersed in cold water; refrigerate and cover their tops loosely with a plastic bag. Be sure to first remove any rubber bands from the asparagus stems. Artichokes will keep for up to 1 week. Asparagus are best cooked and eaten on the day of purchase and better still, on the day of harvest.

When selecting vegetable stalks such as celery and fennel look for firm, plump and crisp heads with no signs of browning. In the refrigerator celery keeps well, up to 1 month, while fennel tends to turn dry and fibrous after 5 days.

Dried alliums, such as onions and garlic, store very well, up to 3 months in a cool, dry place. Choose bulbs with dry, papery skins that feel heavy for their size. Reject any that feel light or are starting to sprout.

When choosing fresh alliums, such as leeks and scallions, look for crisp green tops and firm white bulbs and refrigerate for up to 1 week.

When choosing salad leaves, avoid brown cut ends and wilted or bruised outer leaves. The leaves should be crisp and tightly layered, especially towards the heart. Before storing, always remove and discard damaged leaves. Salad leaves will keep for up to 4 days when refrigerated whole and unwashed and up to 3 days when the leaves are separated, rinsed and dried using a salad spinner. Never tear or cut the leaves until just before serving. To re-crisp limp salad leaves, immerse in icy cold water for 5 minutes, drain and dry in a salad spinner. Chill for 15 minutes in the vegetable crisper drawer of the refrigerator before using.

Watercress is best bought in bunches. Untie and pick out any yellowing or wilting sprigs. Store with the leaves plunged down and the stalks up in a jug of cold water in the refrigerator.

Wherever possible, buy herbs in bunches. Store stems down in a jug of cold water loosely covered with a plastic bag; refrigerate for up to 5 days, changing the water every 2 days. Leaves or small sprigs are best stored loosely wrapped in paper towels and placed in a loosely closed plastic bag in the refrigerator. Stored in this way, most herbs will keep for up to 4 days, but cilantro is best used within 2 days. Select herbs that look lively with no wilted leaves. Your nose is your best guide to fragrant, flavorful herbs.

An easy freshness check for green beans is to fold them in half – they should snap rather than bend. Store refrigerated and use within 5 days. Always buy fresh peas in their pod and shell as close to cooking time as possible. Eat fresh peas without delay as their natural sugars begin to turn to starch after harvesting. Choose shiny, bright green pods that are not too tightly packed, as over mature peas tend to be mealy in texture.

Corn is also best eaten as soon as possible after harvesting. Always buy corn still in its husks. The husks should be green and moist-looking. To test corn kernels for freshness, press a kernel with your fingernail. If newly harvested, it should squirt milky juice. Preferably eat fresh peas and corn on the day of purchase. Otherwise refrigerate and eat the next day.

Vegetable fruits are better not refrigerated as chilling spoils their aroma and texture. A cool, dry room temperature best suits eggplant, squash, tomatoes, avocados and peppers, while even cucumbers do not like excessive cold. A warm kitchen means the vegetable crisper drawer of the refrigerator is your only option, but they are still best eaten within 2-3 days of purchase. When making your selection, choose vegetables that are feel firm, look glossy and are heavy for their size. Check the stem end. It should be fresh looking rather than dried out. To test avocados for ripeness, hold one in the palm of your hand and squeeze very gently; if it yields slightly to pressure, it is ready to eat, otherwise leave to ripen at room temperature or in a closed brown paper bag. Whole winter squashes will keep well for several months in a cool dry place. Once they are cut, press plastic wrap on to the cut surface of squash and refrigerate for up to 1 week.

Avoid roots that are limp or wrinkled. When you can, buy them with their greens still attached. Greens are a good sign of freshness. If they are healthy and moist looking, the roots will be too. To store, cut off any greens, leaving a little stalk, and refrigerate unwashed for up to 2 weeks. Beet and turnip greens are also good to eat; store and cook as for hearty greens. Potatoes are best stored in a cool, dry place protected from the light in a brown paper bag, where they will keep for 2-3 weeks. Avoid any that are sprouting or cracked or that have soft spots or green patches.

Mushrooms should smell pleasantly earthy. Reject any that are withered or slimy. Store loosely packed in brown paper bags so that they can breathe. Refrigerate, but not in the vegetable crisper drawer, which is too moist. Use within 3 days.

For top flavor and fragrance, most fruits are best stored at room temperature. Apples, citrus fruits, kiwi fruit and bananas are good keepers and make the best possible fruit bowl staples, but most fruit, once ripe, should be eaten without delay. Once a week shopping trips are not compatible with good fruit eating. To ripen under-ripe fruit, place in a closed brown paper bag, taking care not to overcrowd.

As a general rule, choose fruits that look plump, feel firm and are heavy for their size. Smell, usually at the stalk end, is the best indication of ripeness. Always check delicate fruits such as berries, figs and stone fruits carefully for signs of dampness or bruising. If you do need to keep these more perishable fruits when ripe, store in a loosely closed plastic bag in the vegetable crisper drawer of the refrigerator, where they will keep for up to 3 days. If you prefer your melon and pineapple chilled, be sure to store in a closed plastic bag as their scent is invasive and will flavor all your dairy products!

# Organic pantry

Keeping a well stocked pantry is the first step to making home cooking easy. Having basic necessities to hand means a simple meal can be on the table without a shopping trip – a far healthier and cheaper alternative to buying take out and convenience foods. One word of warning: don't forget that out of date means out of taste and out of goodness. The shelf life of packaged goods may be longer, but it is not indefinite. Oils turn rancid, dried beans and grains go stale and just because an ingredient is in the freezer doesn't mean it will last forever. Here is a list of essential staples, useful stand-bys and a few extra treats.

## IN THE KITCHEN CUPBOARD

Black peppercorns – a pepper grinder is an essential tool for all home cooks.

Canned beans – wherever possible, choose beans canned in pure water. Chickpeas are well suited to canning. Use to make sustaining soups, nutty salads, and whiz in a food processor with garlic, lemon and olive oil to taste, for a quick-fix dip.

Canned tomatoes – whole plum tomatoes are better value and needn't be messy to chop when you know how. Open the can and snip the tomatoes into pieces with a pair of kitchen scissors. Essential for making pasta sauces and for brightening up winter soups and stews.

Chocolate – guilt-free indulgences (in moderation of course!) are an essential part of our organic ethos - happy people live longer! Organic chocolate is, quite simply, more chocolatey, with a higher cocoa butter solids content and no hydrogenated fats.

Dried fruit – enjoy as chewy, energy-giving sweet treats or in winter compôtes for breakfast and dessert.

Dried herbs – not all herbs are worth buying dry, but oregano, thyme, rosemary and *herbes de provence* bring a taste of the sun to soups, stews and marinades.

Dried pulses – lentils are the most useful variety to have on hand as they require no soaking and can be prepared and ready to eat within 20-40 minutes.

## BULK BUYS

Buying food loose from bulk bins makes perfect sense. You are paying for the food itself, not the packaging, and you can buy as little or as much as you require. The only drawback when buying loose is that it's up to you to keep track of the use-by date. To avoid spoiling good cooking with stale ingredients, store staples in airtight containers in a cool, dark place, do not mix newly purchased ingredients with those already in the pantry, and follow these storage guidelines:

Use grains within 6 months
Use dried beans and pulses
  within 1 year
Use flour within 2 months
Use nuts within 1 month
Use brown rice within 6 months
Use white rice within 1 year

## FREEZING TIPS

Freeze only top-quality fresh foods as soon as possible after purchase. Wrap and pack food carefully to avoid freezer burn. Defrost overnight in the refrigerator. Be sure to label and date all food clearly, and follow the guidelines below on recommended freezing times.

Bread - up to 3 months
Butter - up to 6 months
Fish - up to 3 months
Shellfish - up to 3 months
Meat joints - up to 6 months
Ground or small pieces of meat -
  up to 3 months
Sausages - up to 3 months
Chicken - up to 3 months
Vegetables - up to 1 year
Berries - up to 1 year
Nuts - up to 6 months

Flour - got eggs and milk? With flour as well, crepes or pancakes are just a mix away for simple sweet or savory snacks or meals. Also useful to have on hand for cakes and pastry. If you use infrequently, store in the freezer. This will double its lifespan.

Garlic – if you have olive oil, salt, garlic and pasta in the house, you have a meal. We can't imagine a kitchen without this essential ingredient.

Grains – a wealth of healthful grains are availbale organic. We favor cous-cous, polenta or cornmeal and rice - arborio for risotto, basmati for Asian-style dishes, and brown for maximum nutritional value.

Honey – nature's own sweetener. Organic is the superior choice as most commercial honeys have been blended, filtered and heated to high temperatures.

Mustard – use in dressings, sauces and marinades and as a condiment. Creamy Dijon is our preference.

Oils – we like to keep two grades of olive oil to hand - regular extra virgin for cooking and a premium quality extra virgin for dressing, drizzling and dipping. Keep a neutral tasting oil such as corn, safflower or peanut for stir-frying and for making light dressings.

Olives – for instant nibbles.

Onions – an essential kitchen staple that is the basis of most good savory cooking and, when roasted (see page 110) stands alone as a vegetable in its own right. We like to have red as well as yellow in store. Red have a milder flavor and pretty color.

Pasta – the ultimate staple ingredient for simple sustaining supper fare. Choose Italian and stock a selection of shapes and sizes.

Peanut butter – who could be without it? Choose stone-ground for the fullest flavor.

Pesto – use to sauce pasta, enrich vegetable soups and stews, and as a topping for grilled chicken, meat or fish. Refrigerate after opening.

Porridge oats – still the best way to start a cold winter's day.

Salt – food lovers know that the quality of salt matters. Choose good quality sea salt which is unrefined, from unpolluted sources and harvested using traditional methods. We like to keep natural kosher and fine salt to hand.

Shoyu – Japanese soy sauce. Sweeter, lighter and less salty than regular soy.

Spices – the ideal is to buy spices whole and to crush them to order as this allows them to keep their fragrance and flavor longer. Alternatively, renew your supply every six months. Our essentials for the spice pantry are red pepper flakes, paprika, cumin, coriander, turmeric, cinnamon and nutmeg.

Tapenade – to spread on bruschetta (see page 54) for an easy opener. Refrigerate after opening.

Tomato ketchup – a family necessity. Organic ketchups are all-natural, taste more of real tomatoes. They are more tangy and less sweet.

Vinegar – red wine and balsamic are essential necessities for food lovers. Red wine vinegar is the king of French dressings. A drizzle of balsamic vinegar adds depth of flavor to grills and roasts pre and post cooking.

**Wine** – make deliciously simple sauces for meat by adding half a glass to the pan after frying. Cook down the pan juices until syrupy. Also essential for slow-cooked stews and braises, and of course for a glass as you cook.

## IN THE REFRIGERATOR

**Butter** – keep your main supply in the freezer for optimum freshness and the purest flavor.

**Cheese** – PARMESAN stores well in a piece that weighs no more than 8-10oz (250 - 300g), wrapped in foil and kept in the warmest part of the refrigerator. Combined with butter, black pepper and pasta, grated parmesan provides a simple supper solution. A hard cheese that melts well, such as CHEDDAR or GRUYERE is also a must-have. Cut into dice, it will add richness to winter vegetable soups and sustenance to a crisp green leaf salad. When grated, it is a perfect partner to eggs, especially omelettes or scrambled.

**Eggs** – the ultimate in convenience food. A few eggs combined with a couple of staple ingredients will give you a meal in minutes.

**Greens** – whether hearty or tender, try to always have something green to hand.

**Lemons** – as organic lemons are not waxed or treated with post harvest sprays, it is important to store them in the refrigerator. Lemon wedges are the freshest of natural garnishes for simple grilled chicken, meat or fish.

**Mayonnaise** – a sandwich essential. Organic mayos are made with real eggs, pure oil and natural seasonings only.

**Milk** – whether cow's or soy, a kitchen is not stocked without it.

**Natural yogurt** – for breakfast or desserts, or for a low-fat creamy garnish in soups or with pastries.

## IN THE FREEZER

**Berries** – buy in bags or freeze your own at peak season. Great for smoothies, sorbets, fruit fools and quick-fix sauces (see page 116).

**Bread** – sliced for toast and smaller whole loaves like baguette for putting straight into the oven from the freezer and serving warm.

**Butter** – individual sticks in foil. Wrap and freeze.

**Ginger** – stock up on organic fresh ginger when you can. Cut off chunks, peel and grate frozen as needed.

**Ice-cream** – with no artificial flavorings or additives, organic ice cream is the next best thing to home made. For impromptu desserts, with or without quick-fix sauces (see page 116).

**Nuts** – pine nuts, almonds and walnuts or pecans get our vote. Their shelf life is limited so we prefer to freeze them. Toast nuts in a dry pan over medium low heat until golden and serve as nutty nibbles, use to add crunch to salads or sprinkle over honey drizzled yogurt.

**Peas** – make a classic pasta sauce with butter as well as children's favorite green vegetable. Always choose *petis pois*.

**Sausages** – stock up on best quality sausages when you can.

**Spinach** – your green leaf fix on ice. Bags of loose frozen leaves are our preference.

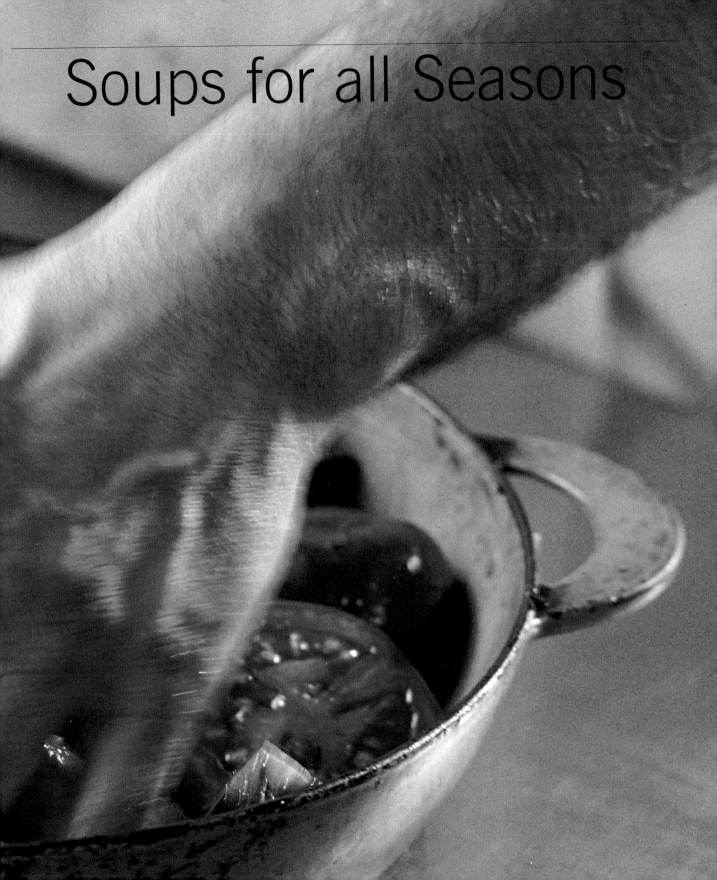

# Soups for all Seasons

**SERVES 4**

3 tbsp extra virgin olive oil

2 slices bacon, chopped, optional

1 medium onion, finely chopped

2 stalks celery, diced

1 carrot, diced

4 garlic cloves, finely sliced

¼ tsp finely chopped fresh rosemary or a pinch of dried, crumbled rosemary

1 medium potato, diced

10oz (300g) greens (see opposite), coarsely chopped

14oz (400g) can italian plum tomatoes, chopped

14oz (400g) can beans (see opposite), drained and rinsed

6 cups chicken or vegetable stock

salt, black pepper

additional extra virgin olive oil to drizzle

¼ cup freshly grated parmesan to serve

# Tuscan Vegetable Soup with Greens and Beans

• Heat the oil in a heavy-based pot. Add the bacon, if using, onion, celery, carrot, garlic, rosemary, potato and greens. Cook, stirring frequently, over medium low heat until the onions soften and the greens wilt, 10 minutes.

• Turn the heat to medium. Add the tomatoes and cook, stirring occasionally, until just thickened, 10 minutes. Add the beans and stock. Bring to a boil.

• Adjust the heat, partially cover and simmer gently until the vegetables are very tender, 30 minutes. The soup should be fairly thick, but be prepared to add water to thin if necessary. Add salt and pepper to taste. Ladle into warm bowls. Drizzle with oil and sprinkle with parmesan. Serve hot.

**VARIATION**

## Provençal Vegetable Soup with Greens and Beans

Make the soup as directed, adding a small handful of broken up spaghetti to the soup 10-12 minutes before the end of simmering time. Simmer until the pasta is tender. Remove the soup from the heat and stir in 4 tbsp basil pesto. Ladle into warm bowls and serve hot.

**WHICH GREENS?**

Choose from kale, savoy cabbage, swiss chard, broccoli rabe, spring greens or cavolo nero.

**WHICH BEANS?**

You can be equally inspirational about your choice of bean in this soul-satisfying soup. For a delicate flavor and creamy texture, choose from cannellini, dried white or flageolet beans.

For a firmer bite and a slightly nutty taste, choose either lima beans or chickpeas.

# Potato, Garlic and Parsley **Soup**

• Heat the oil or butter in a heavy-based pot. Add the potato slices, onion and garlic. Cook, stirring occasionally, over medium heat until the onions are softened, 10 minutes.

• Add half the chopped parsley and the stock. Bring to a boil. Adjust the heat, partially cover and simmer gently until the potatoes are tender, 30 minutes. Add the remaining parsley.

• For a creamy soup, leave to cool slightly and purée until smooth with a hand blender or in a food processor. Alternatively, leave the soup chunky. Stir in the milk or cream, if using. Thin with water as needed. Add salt and pepper to taste. Ladle into warm bowls and serve hot.

**VARIATIONS**

## Potato, Garlic and Leek Soup

Omit the parsley and replace half the potatoes with 3 medium, finely sliced leeks. Cook as directed.

## Potato, Garlic and Fennel Soup

Omit the parsley and replace half the potatoes with 2 medium, finely sliced fennel bulbs. Cook and finish as directed.

**SERVES 4**

2 tbsp extra virgin olive oil or butter
1½ lb (750g) potatoes, quartered and finely sliced
1 onion, finely chopped
8 garlic cloves, finely sliced
2 handfuls fresh parsley, chopped
6 cups chicken or vegetable stock
½ cup milk or heavy cream, optional
salt, black pepper

**COOK'S TIP**

Organic fresh parsley - especially flat-leaf - is not always easy to find. Luckily, it freezes well; chop and store in an airtight container and scoop out straight from the freezer as needed.

**HEALTH BITE**

Parsley tastes good, looks good and is good for you! This herbal superfood is rich in vitamins A and C as well as calcium, iron and folic acid. Parsley should be added at the end of the cooking time to preserve both its vivid green color and its optimum nutritional value.

**SERVES 4**

2 tbsp olive oil or butter
1 large onion, finely chopped
4 garlic cloves, crushed
2 tbsp freshly grated ginger
1 tsp ground cumin
1 tsp ground coriander
¼ tsp cayenne pepper
1½ lb (750g) carrots, roughly
   chopped
1 medium potato, roughly
   chopped
6 cups chicken or vegetable
   stock
1 tsp honey
2 tbsp lemon or orange juice
salt, black pepper

**HEALTH BITE**
Chock-full of beta carotene,
carrots cleanse, alkalize, nourish and stimulate many body
systems, while supplying a
great-tasting, easy-to-digest
dose of vitamins and minerals.

# Moroccan Spiced
# Carrot Soup

• Heat the oil or butter in a heavy-based pot. Add the onion, garlic, ginger, cumin, coriander, cayenne, carrot and potato and cook, stirring occasionally, over medium low heat until the vegetables are soft, 10 minutes.
• Turn the heat to medium. Add the stock and bring to a boil. Adjust the heat, partially cover and simmer gently until the potato is tender, 30 minutes.
• Leave to cool slightly. Purée until smooth with a hand blender or in a food processor. Stir in honey and lemon or orange juice. Thin with water as needed. Add salt and pepper to taste. Ladle into warm bowls and serve hot.

**VARIATION**
## Carrot and Parsnip Soup with Ginger
Omit the cumin, coriander and cayenne. Replace half the carrots with 2 chopped medium parsnips. Cook as directed.

# Pick-Me-Up
# Miso Tofu Soup

• Place the miso in a bowl and stir in a little of the water to dilute to a thick cream. Set aside.

• Place the remaining water in a pan and bring to a boil. Lower the heat and add the tofu, mushrooms and carrots. Simmer gently until the tofu rises to the surface, 3 minutes.

• Remove from the heat and stir in the diluted miso. Ladle into warmed bowls and sprinkle with scallions and sesame oil. Serve hot.

### WHICH MISO?

Miso is available in many varieties that vary in color, texture and saltiness, but basically divides into 2 types. Red miso is thicker and saltier and is traditionally used in winter soups. White miso is more delicate and sweeter, and is preferred for lighter, summer soups.

**SERVES 4**

3 tbsp miso (see opposite)
4 cups water
2½ oz (75g) firm tofu, diced
4 button mushrooms, finely sliced
½ carrot, cut into fine matchsticks
2 scallions, finely sliced
a few drops toasted sesame oil

### HEALTH BITE

Miso is a protein-rich fermented soy bean paste. Considered in Japan as a gift from the gods, it has readily digestible amino acids, fatty acids and simple sugars. Never boil miso, as boiling destroys its living enzymes.

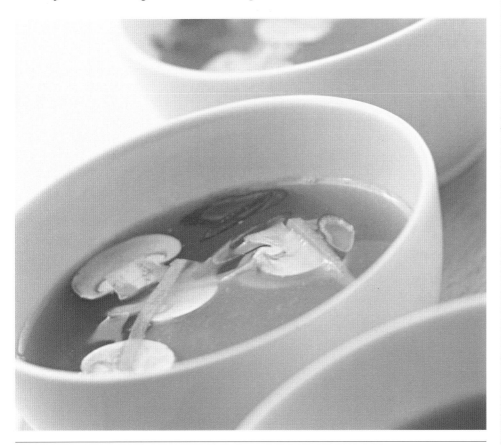

# **Roast** Red Pepper and Tomato **Soup** with Basil

**SERVES 4**

4¼ lb (2kg) ripe tomatoes,
  halved
2 red bell peppers, cored,
  seeded and quartered
2 red onions, quartered
1 handful fresh basil, leaves
  and stalks torn
4 garlic cloves, crushed
1 tbsp balsamic vinegar
¼ cup extra virgin olive oil
¼ tsp red pepper flakes
salt, black pepper
extra torn fresh basil leaves
  to serve

**COOK'S TIP**
Both bell peppers and tomatoes are best stored at room temperature, as refrigeration spoils their texture and aroma.

**HEALTH BITE**
The bright red or orange color of fruits or vegetables generally indicates high beta-carotene and vitamin C content, and red bell peppers and ripe tomatoes are no exception to the rule.

• Preheat oven to 400°F (200°C).
• Place the tomatoes cut side up with the peppers and onions in a roasting pan. Scatter with basil. Combine garlic, vinegar and oil and drizzle over the tomatoes, peppers and onions. Sprinkle with red pepper flakes, salt and pepper. Roast until very soft and wilted, 1 hour.
• Leave to cool slightly. Purée, leaving a little texture, with a hand blender or in a food processor. The soup should be fairly thick, but be prepared to thin with water if necessary. Add salt and pepper to taste. Ladle into warm bowls and sprinkle with extra basil. Serve hot or at room temperature.

# Spiced Green Lentil Soup with Spinach and Lemon

**SERVES 4**

2 tbsp extra virgin olive oil
1 onion, finely chopped
4 garlic cloves, crushed
3 celery stalks, diced
2 medium potatoes, diced
1 tsp ground cumin
8oz (250g) green lentils
6 cups chicken or
   vegetable stock
1lb (500g) spinach or swiss
   chard, coarsely chopped
2 tbsp lemon juice
salt, black pepper

**HEALTH BITE**
An essential part of any health smart diet plan, lentils are high protein, high fiber and iron rich. They are also an excellent source of valuable B vitamins.

• Heat the oil in a heavy-based pot. Add the onion, garlic, celery, potato and cumin and cook, stirring frequently, over medium low heat until the potato is tender, 10 minutes.
• Increase the heat to medium. Add the lentils and stock and bring to a boil. Adjust the heat, partially cover and simmer gently until the lentils are tender, 20-30 minutes.
• Add the spinach or chard and cook until wilted but still bright green, 3 minutes. Add the lemon juice and salt and pepper to taste. Ladle into warm bowls and serve hot.

**VARIATION**
## Hearty Green Lentil Soup with Bacon and Red Wine Vinegar

Omit the ground cumin. Add 4 chopped bacon slices with the onion, celery and potato to the pot. Cook as directed. Replace the lemon juice with 1 tbsp red wine vinegar.

# Ginger Squash Soup

**SERVES 4**

2 tbsp corn oil

2lb (1kg) orange-fleshed
winter squash, peeled,
seeded and cut first into
wedges and then into
chunks

1 medium potato, quartered
and finely sliced

1 medium leek, finely sliced

4 garlic cloves, crushed

2 tbsp freshly grated ginger

6 cups vegetable stock or
water

lemon or lime juice to taste

salt, black pepper

**COOK'S TIP**

Look for squashes that are heavy
for their size, with thick, hard
skins showing no blemishes or
bruises. In general, the harder the
skins, the riper - and sweeter - the
squash. Winter squash store well,
and in fact generally improve after
a few weeks of storage.

**HEALTH BITE**

The most medicinal of spices,
ginger is an aromatic stimulant and
is thought to promote overall
circulation of energy in the body. It
can also aid digestion, ease nausea
and fight coughs and colds.

• Heat the oil in a heavy based pot. Add the squash, potato, leek, garlic and ginger and cook, stirring occasionally, over medium heat until the vegetables are soft, 10 minutes.

• Add the stock and bring to a boil. Adjust the heat, partially cover and simmer gently until the potato is tender, 30 minutes.

• Add lemon or lime juice and salt and pepper to taste. Ladle into warm bowls and serve hot.

**VARIATIONS**

## Ginger Squash Soup with Lemon Grass and Coconut

Add the finely chopped tender stem of 1 lemon grass stalk to the pot with the vegetables and cook as directed. When the vegetables are tender, stir in ½ cup canned coconut milk. Heat through and proceed as directed.

**WHICH SQUASH?**

## Butternut or hubbard squash would be our preference, but any squash with deep orange flesh will be rich in flavor.

# Whole Meal Salads

# Crisp Leaf Salad with Apple, Blue Cheese and Walnuts

- For the dressing, mix together vinegar and oil until blended. Add salt and pepper to taste.
- Place the walnut pieces in a dry pan over a medium heat. Toast, shaking the pan occasionally, until browned, 5 minutes. Remove from the pan and leave to cool.
- Place the salad leaves, apple and cucumber in a large bowl. Add dressing and toss to coat. Arrange on a serving dish or plates. Sprinkle with walnuts and cheese. Serve immediately.

**VARIATION**

## Bitter Leaf Salad with Pear, Blue Cheese & Walnuts

Omit the crisp salad leaves and replace with 4 handfuls bitter leaves, such as frisée, chicory, watercress or arugula. Omit apples and replace with 2 pears. Omit cucumber and replace with 1 fennel bulb. Proceed as directed.

# Mozzarella, Tomato and Avocado Salad with Basil

- Layer the tomatoes, avocado and mozzarella on a large serving dish or individual plates, sprinkling with salt and pepper in between the layers. Drizzle over lemon juice and oil. Scatter with basil and serve immediately.

---

**SERVES 4**

FOR THE DRESSING
2 tbsp red wine vinegar
¼ cup extra virgin olive oil
salt, black pepper

½ cup walnut pieces
4 handfuls crisp salad leaves such as boston or iceberg, torn
2 apples, cut into ¾ in (2cm) pieces
1 cucumber, cut into ¾ in (2cm) cubes
1 cup blue cheese, crumbled

**HEALTH BITE**
The king of fruit and great detoxifiers, apples are loaded with pectin, a soluble fiber that sweeps toxins out of the body. They are also potassium rich and highly alkaline. An apple a day really can help keep the doctor away!

**SERVES 4**
4 ripe tomatoes, sliced
2 avocados, halved and sliced crosswise
8oz (250g) mozzarella, sliced
salt, black pepper
1 tbsp lemon juice
3 tbsp extra virgin olive oil
1 handful fresh basil leaves, torn

**COOK'S TIP**
Never store ripe tomatoes in the refrigerator, as this spoils their texture and aroma. It is far better to eat them immediately, at the height of their ripeness, freshness and goodness.

**HEALTH BITE**
Eaten raw, ripe and fresh, tomatoes are a powerhouse of vitamin C. They are also rich in lycopene, an antioxidant that assists in preventing heart disease and cancer.

# **Grilled** Vegetable Platter with Pesto **Dressing**

• For the dressing, place the pine nuts or almonds in a dry pan over medium heat. Toast, stirring frequently, until golden and fragrant, 10 minutes. Remove from the pan immediately and leave to cool. Place pine nuts or almonds, basil or parsley, garlic and oil in a food processor; pulse until smooth. Add salt and pepper to taste.

• Preheat an outdoor grill or ridged cast-iron grill pan to medium hot.

• Brush the vegetables with olive oil and sprinkle with salt and pepper. Grill, turning once or twice, until lightly charred and tender.

• Toss with pesto dressing. Arrange on a large serving dish. Serve hot or at room temperature.

**WHICH VEGETABLES?**

Tender summer vegetables are best for grilling. Choose from:

red, yellow or orange bell peppers, quartered

tomatoes, ripe, firm and halved

eggplant, cut into ½ in (1cm) thick rounds

red onions, cut into ¾ in (2cm) thick rounds

zucchini, cut lengthwise into ½ in (1cm) thick slices

asparagus, woody end snapped off

scallions, whole

summer squash, cut into wedges

**SERVES 4**

FOR THE PESTO DRESSING
2 tbsp pine nuts or almonds
2 handfuls fresh basil or
 flat-leaf parsley
1 garlic clove, crushed
6 tbsp extra virgin olive oil
salt, black pepper

2lb (1kg) mixed vegetables
 (see opposite)
extra virgin olive oil
salt, black pepper

**COOK'S TIP**
You can grill the vegetables up to 6 hours in advance. Cover and store at room temperature. Refrigeration spoils their smoky flavor.

**SERVES 4**
FOR THE DRESSING
1 tsp grainy dijon mustard
1 tsp horseradish sauce
1 tsp sugar
2 tbsp white wine vinegar
¼ cup extra virgin olive oil
salt, black pepper

1 bunch watercress
2 heads chicory, separated
  into leaves
½ red onion, finely sliced
6oz (175g) smoked salmon,
  thinly sliced
black pepper

**HEALTH BITE**
Like other dark green leafy vegetables, watercress is rich in
anti-carcinogenic antioxidants.

# Watercress, Chicory and Smoked Salmon Salad with Horseradish Dressing

• For the dressing, mix together the mustard, horseradish, sugar, vinegar and oil until thick and smooth. Add salt and pepper to taste.
• Place the watercress, chicory and red onion in a large bowl. Add the dressing and toss to coat. Arrange on a serving dish or plates. Lay the salmon slices on top. Sprinkle with pepper. Serve immediately.

**VARIATION**
## Watercress and Chicory Salad with Smoked Trout
Replace smoked salmon with 2 fillets of smoked trout, flaked. Proceed as directed.

# French Lentil Salad with Baby Spinach

• Place the lentils in a large pan with cold water to cover by 2in (5cm). Bring to a boil. Adjust heat and simmer until the lentils are tender, 20-30 minutes.
• Drain and place the lentils in a large bowl with the garlic, mustard, vinegar, oil and onion. Mix well. Add salt and pepper to taste. Just before serving, add parsley and spinach and toss to combine. Serve warm or at room temperature.

**VARIATION**

## French Lentil Salad with Bitter Leaves

Omit baby spinach leaves and replace with 2 heads chicory, leaves separated, or 1 medium radicchio, leaves torn into bite-sized pieces, or 4 handfuls frisée, torn. Proceed as directed.

# Bacon, Avocado and Goat Cheese Salad with Dijon Dressing

• Preheat the oven to 350°F (180°C).
• For the dressing, mix together mustard, vinegar and olive oil until thick and smooth. Add salt and pepper to taste.
• Place the bacon on a foil-lined baking tray. Cook until crisp and golden, 10-15 minutes. Drain on paper towels. Using kitchen scissors, snip the bacon into ¾ in (2cm) pieces.
• Place the bacon, spinach and avocado in a large bowl. Add the dressing and toss to coat. Arrange on a serving dish or plates. Top with goat cheese. Serve immediately.

---

**SERVES 4**

8oz (250g) french puy or green lentils
2 garlic cloves, crushed
1 tsp creamy dijon mustard
2 tbsp red wine vinegar
¼ cup extra virgin olive oil
1 small red onion, finely sliced
salt, black pepper
2 tbsp chopped fresh parsley
4 handfuls baby spinach leaves, washed

**COOK'S TIP**
Cook lentils up to 1 day in advance, but for maximum flavor, dress them while they are still hot. Cover and refrigerate, but return to room temperature before serving. Puy lentils are the best choice for salads as they hold their shape when cooked.

**SERVES 4**
FOR THE DRESSING
2 tsp dijon-style mustard
2 tbsp balsamic vinegar
¼ cup extra virgin olive oil
salt, black pepper

12 slices bacon
4 large handfuls baby spinach leaves, washed
2 avocados, quartered and sliced
4oz (125g) goat cheese, diced

**COOK'S TIP**
There is no need to restrict this salad to baby spinach. Crisp salad leaves are also delicious. Tear into bite-sized pieces.

**HEALTH BITE**
Easily digestible, with a perfect pH balance, avocados are packed with minerals that regulate body function.

# Roast Pepper, Artichoke and Feta Salad with Arugula

**SERVES 4**

2 red bell peppers
1 small red onion, finely sliced
1 – 10oz (300g) jar artichoke hearts in oil, drained and quartered
4 tomatoes, quartered, seeded and halved
4oz (125g) feta cheese, diced
1 tbsp capers, drained and rinsed
4 handfuls arugula
1 tbsp brown rice vinegar
3 tbsp extra virgin olive oil
salt, black pepper

**COOK'S TIP**

You can roast and peel the peppers up to 3 days in advance. Cover and refrigerate, but return to room temperature before serving. Although peppery arugula is our preference, other salad greens work well. Try sprigs of fresh flat-leaf parsley or watercress, or tear salad leaves into bite-sized pieces. You can assemble and dress the salad up to 1 day in advance, but add the arugula just before serving.

• Roast the peppers under a hot grill, turning as needed, until charred and wrinkled on all sides, 10-15 minutes. Place in a plastic bag or a bowl with a plate on top and leave until cool. The steam released by the peppers as they cool will loosen the skin.

• Uncover the cooled peppers. Peel off the charred skin, scraping off any remaining bits of skin. Cut the peppers into quarters and remove the core. Scrape away the seeds and discard. Cut the quarters into 1in (2.5cm) pieces.

• Place the pepper, onion, artichoke hearts, tomatoes, feta, capers, arugula, vinegar and oil in a large bowl. Toss to coat. Add salt and pepper to taste. Serve immediately.

**ROAST PEPPER SALAD ADD-ONS**

Add 2 tbsp black olives to the salad. Finish as directed.

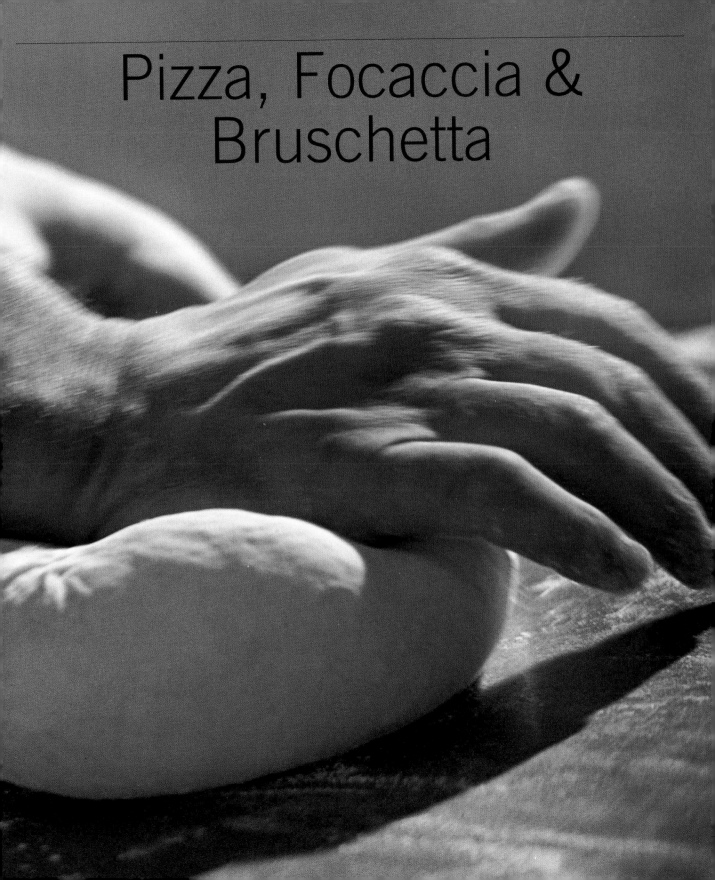

# Pizza, Focaccia & Bruschetta

# Olive Oil Rich Dough

- Place the flour and salt in a large bowl. Make a well in the center and add the water. Sprinkle over the yeast and leave to stand until softened, 5 minutes. Stir to dissolve.
- Draw in flour from the sides to make a sticky dough. Turn out on to a lightly floured surface. Knead to a smooth, soft dough. Try not to add too much extra flour, as the dough will firm up as you knead it.
- Place the dough in an oiled bowl and cover. Leave to rise until doubled in size, about 1-1½ hours. Deflate the dough by pressing down with the palm of your hand. The dough is now ready for shaping into pizza bases (see below) or focaccia (see page 53).

# Pizza Bases

- Divide the dough into 4 equal-sized pieces. Shape each piece into a ball, cover with a cloth and set aside for 10 minutes. This allows the dough to rest, making it easier to stretch. The shaped dough balls can stand covered with a cloth for up to 1 hour before shaping, topping and baking.
- Place a dough ball on a lightly floured surface. Roll out the dough with a rolling pin to a 12in (30cm) round about ¼in (5mm) thick. Turn the dough over several times as you roll it, to prevent it from sticking or shrinking. If the dough resists stretching, leave it to rest again for 3 minutes. Don't worry if the dough is not perfectly round.
- Dust a baking tray with coarse cornmeal. Place a shaped dough round on the dusted baking tray.

**MAKES ENOUGH DOUGH FOR 4 PIZZAS OR 1 FOCACCIA**
3½ cups all-purpose flour, additional for dusting
1 tsp salt
1 cup tepid water
1 tsp dried active yeast
1½ tbsp olive oil

**COOK'S TIP**
The dough will be quite sticky but try to resist working in too much extra flour as you knead. A moist dough bakes to a light pizza base with a crisp crust and an airy crumb, while a stiff dough willl make heavy bases.

**MAKES 4 - 12in (30cm) PIZZA BASES**
1 recipe olive oil rich dough (see above)
flour and coarse cornmeal for sprinkling

# Spinach, Blue Cheese and Pine Nut **Pizza**

- Adjust your racks to the top of the oven. Place pizza stone or baking sheet in the oven and preheat the oven to as hot as possible, allowing 30 minutes.
- For the tomato sauce, place the tomatoes and their juice in a food processor; pulse until smooth.
- If using fresh spinach, rinse well. Place in a large pan with the water still clinging to the leaves. Cook over high heat, stirring frequently, until wilted and bright green, 3-5 minutes. Drain and rinse in cold water. With your hands, squeeze spinach to remove excess water.
- Shape one pizza and place on a dusted baking sheet (see page 47). Spread pizza base evenly with tomato sauce. Cover with an even layer of spinach. Sprinkle with blue cheese, pine nuts, salt and pepper. Drizzle over oil.
- Slide the pizza off the baking sheet onto the stone, if using, or onto the preheated baking sheet in the oven (see cook's tip). Bake until the crust is crisp and golden, 5-10 minutes. Serve immediately.
- Repeat with the remaining toppings and pizzas.

**MAKES 4 PIZZAS**

FOR THE PIZZA
1 recipe olive oil rich dough (see page 47)
coarse cornmeal for sprinkling

FOR THE TOMATO SAUCE
14oz (400g) can italian plum tomatoes, whole not chopped

FOR THE TOPPING
1½ lb (750g) fresh spinach, or 10oz (300g) frozen spinach, defrosted and squeezed dry
1½ cups blue cheese, preferably gorgonzola, crumbled
4 tbsp pine nuts
salt, black pepper
2 tbsp extra virgin olive oil

**COOK'S TIP**
We highly recommend using a pizza stone or a preheated heavy baking sheet. A stone provides an intense heat to cook the crust quickly and evenly.
To transfer the pizza to the stone with ease, make sure you dust the baking sheet with enough cornmeal. Shake the sheet back and forwards in order to loosen and to allow the pizza to slide off easily. If it doesn't slide off, remove and dust again. Place the edge of the baking sheet on to the edge of the stone. With a sharp yank, pull away the baking sheet from under the pizza.

# Grilled Eggplant Pizza with Basil

**MAKES 4 PIZZAS**

1 medium eggplant, cut into
¼ in (5mm) thick slices

2 tbsp extra virgin olive oil,
plus additional for brushing
and drizzling

2 garlic cloves, crushed

1 recipe olive oil rich dough
(see page 47)

½ medium red onion, finely
sliced

4oz (125g) mozzarella, finely
sliced

2 ripe tomatoes, cut into ¼ in
(5mm) thick slices

salt, black pepper

1 handful fresh basil leaves,
torn

**COOK'S TIP**

For the crispest crusts, it's best to
bake the pizzas one at a time.
When the first pizza is in the oven,
start topping the second, so, when
the first is ready to eat, the second
will be ready to bake. Then, by the
time you have finished eating the
first, the second will be ready.
Pizza is best eaten as soon as it
comes out of the oven as the crust
will soften as it cools.

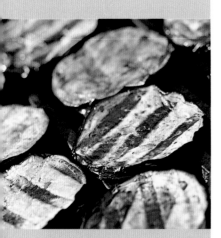

• Adjust your racks to the top of the oven. Place pizza stone or baking sheet in the oven and preheat the oven to as hot as possible, allowing 30 minutes.

• Preheat a ridged cast-iron grill pan or broiler. Brush the eggplant slices on both sides with olive oil. Grill or broil until lightly charred and tender, 5 minutes per side.

• Combine the garlic and the oil.

• Shape one pizza and place on a dusted baking sheet (see page 47). Brush one pizza base with garlic oil.

• Arrange red onion slices, mozzarella slices, eggplant slices and tomato slices in a even layers over the pizza base. Sprinkle with salt and pepper. Drizzle over a little oil.

• Slide the pizza off the baking sheet onto the stone, if using, or the baking sheet in the oven (see cook's tip on page 49). Alternatively, place the baking sheet on a rack in the oven. Bake until the crust is crisp and golden, 5-10 minutes. Serve immediately.

• Repeat with the remaining toppings and pizzas.

**VARIATION**

## Red Pepper and Oregano Pizza

Omit eggplant, tomatoes and basil. Replace with 2 red bell peppers cut into fine strips. Combine the pepper strips, red onion slices, crushed garlic, 2 tbsp oil and salt and pepper to taste. Arrange mozzarella over one pizza base in a single layer. Spread pepper mixture evenly over the mozzarella. Sprinkle over a pinch each dried oregano and red pepper flakes. Bake as directed. Scatter with basil and serve immediately. Repeat with the remaining toppings and pizza bases.

# Simple Olive Oil Focaccia

**MAKES 1 FOCACCIA**
1 recipe olive oil rich dough
(see page 47)
1 tsp kosher salt
2 tbsp additional extra virgin
olive oil

**ESSENTIAL EQUIPMENT**
*13 x 9in (33 x 23cm) oven
tray*

**COOK'S TIP**
You can bake the focaccia up to
1 day in advance. Leave to cool
completely before storing in a
loosely closed plastic bag at room
temperature. Warm through in a
preheated 300°F (150°C) oven
for 15 minutes before serving.

• Press the dough into the oiled oven sheet. Dimple the dough all over with your fingertips, making dents ½in (1cm) deep. Cover with a cloth and leave to rise until doubled in thickness, 45 minutes.

• Preheat the oven to 400°F (200°C).

• Sprinkle the dough with salt and bake until golden and hollow-sounding when tapped underneath, 30 - 40 minutes. Drizzle over the additional oil. Cool on a wire rack.

**VARIATIONS**

## Rosemary Focaccia

Follow recipe for dough on page 47, adding 2 tsp finely chopped fresh rosemary or 1 tsp crumbled dried rosemary to the flour with the salt. Proceed as directed. Just before baking, decorate the focaccia with fresh rosemary leaves.

## Olive Focaccia

Follow recipe for dough on page 47, kneading 5oz (150g) pitted black or green olives into the dough towards the end of kneading. Proceed as directed.

## Onion Focaccia

Cut 1 halved onion into very fine slices. Scatter the shaped dough with onion slices. Proceed as directed.

# Olive Oil Bruschetta with Red Pepper and Almond Pesto

**SERVES 4**

FOR THE PESTO
2 large red bell peppers
3 tbsp whole almonds
2 garlic cloves
¼ tsp red pepper flakes
½ tsp balsamic vinegar
4 tbsp extra virgin olive oil
salt, black pepper

FOR THE BRUSCHETTA
4 slices day-old bread, cut
   into ½ in (1cm) thick slices
1 garlic clove, halved
extra virgin olive oil

**COOK'S TIP**
You can make the pesto up to 3
days in advance. Cover and
refrigerate, but return to room
temperature before serving.

• Roast peppers under a hot broiler, turning as needed, until charred and wrinkled on all sides, 10-15 minutes. Place in a plastic bag or a bowl with a plate on top and leave until cool. The steam released by the peppers as they cool will loosen the skin. Uncover the cooled peppers. Peel of the charred skin, scraping off any remaining bits of skin. Cut the peppers into quarters and remove the core. Scrape away seeds and discard.

• Place the almonds in a dry pan over medium heat. Toast, stirring frequently, until golden and fragrant, 10 minutes. Remove the almonds from the pan immediately. Place the roast peppers, garlic, almonds, red pepper flakes, vinegar and oil in a food processor; pulse until smooth. Add salt and pepper to taste.

• To make the bruschetta, toast the bread on a preheated ridged cast-iron grill pan or outdoor grill until crisp and striped, 2 minutes per side. Alternatively, use a preheated overhead broiler. Rub one side of each slice with the cut garlic and drizzle over olive oil.

• Spread the pepper and almond pesto over the bruschetta. Serve at room temperature.

**SERVES 4**

FOR THE BRUSCHETTA

4 slices day-old bread, cut
  into ½ in (1cm) thick slices
1 garlic clove, halved
extra virgin olive oil

**MORE TOPPINGS FOR OLIVE OIL BRUSCHETTA**

## Bruschetta with Avocado Goat Cheese

Prepare avocado yogurt dressing (see page 108), replacing yogurt with 4oz (125g) fresh creamy goat cheese. Make bruschetta as directed on page 54. Spread avocado goat cheese over the bruschetta. Serve at room temperature.

## Bruschetta with Roast Cherry Tomatoes

Prepare 1 recipe Roast Cherry Tomato Sauce (see page 68). Make bruschetta as directed on page 54. Spread tomatoes over the bruschetta. Serve at room temperature.

## Bruschetta with Marinated White Beans

Prepare 1 recipe Marinated Beans with Olive Oil, Lemon and Chili (see page 101). Mash the beans with a wooden spoon to make a rough purée. Make bruschetta as directed on page 54. Spread bean mixture over the bruschetta. Serve at room temperature.

## Bruschetta with Pan-Fried Mushrooms

Prepare 1 recipe Pan-Fried Mushrooms (see page 60). Make bruschetta as directed on page 54. Spread mushrooms over the bruschetta. Serve immediately.

# What's for Dinner?

# Polenta

**SERVES 4**
FOR THE POLENTA

3¾ cups water

1¼ cups polenta or coarse
cornmeal

1 tsp salt

½ tsp black pepper

**COOK'S TIP**
You can make the polenta up to 3
days in advance. Wrap in plastic
wrap and refrigerate.

• Bring the water to a boil in a heavy based pot. Turn heat to medium and gradually pour in the polenta, stirring constantly. Add salt and turn heat to low. Cook, stirring constantly, until the polenta is very thick and pulls away from the sides of the pot, 15 minutes.

• Add pepper and mix-ins (see below), if using. Pour the hot polenta onto an oiled baking sheet and spread into a round about 12in (30cm) in diameter and ½in (1cm) thick. Leave to cool until set.

POLENTA MIX-INS

For added flavor, stir in any or a combination of 2 crushed garlic cloves, 4 tbsp freshly grated parmesan, 2 tbsp chopped fresh herbs, such as parsley, basil, thyme or rosemary.

## Crisp Polenta with Pan-Fried Mushrooms

**SERVES 4**
FOR THE MUSHROOMS

2 tbsp extra virgin olive oil

2 shallots

1 garlic clove, chopped

1lb (500g) mushrooms,
shiitake, portabella, cremini,
oyster or any combination

½ cup crème fraîche
or heavy cream

1 recipe polenta (see above)

2 tbsp butter

• Preheat an overhead broiler.

• Heat the oil in a heavy skillet. Add shallots, garlic and mushrooms and cook, stirring constantly, over high heat until mushrooms wilt and start to crisp, 5 minutes. Add crème fraîche or cream and cook until just thickened, 2 minutes.

• Cut the polenta into 8 wedges. Dot the wedges with butter. Broil until crisp and golden, 5-10 minutes. Serve immediately with the hot mushrooms.

## Crisp Polenta with Blue Cheese and Butter

**SERVES 4**

1 recipe polenta (see above)

2 tbsp butter

4 tbsp freshly grated
parmesan

1¼ cups blue cheese,
preferably gorgonzola,
crumbled

• Preheat an overhead broiler.

• Cut the polenta into 8 wedges. Dot the wedges with butter and sprinkle with parmesan. Broil until crisp and golden, 5-10 minutes. Sprinkle with gorgonzola and serve immediately.

**SERVES 4**

4oz (125g) fresh creamy
  goat cheese
2 tbsp finely chopped
  fresh herbs (see opposite)
1 garlic clove, crushed
salt, black pepper
4 boneless chicken breast
  halves (with skins)
2 tbsp extra virgin olive oil

**COOK'S TIP**

You can prepare the chicken
breast halves up to 1 day in
advance. Wrap in plastic wrap
and refrigerate. If possible, leave
to stand at room temperature for
20 minutes before cooking.

# **Pan-Roast** Chicken with Herbed Goat Cheese

- Preheat the oven to 400°F (200°C).
- Combine the goat cheese, herbs and garlic. Add salt and pepper to taste.
- With one hand on a chicken breast half to hold it in place, slice through the middle horizontally to cut almost in half. Open out flat. Spread a quarter of the herbed mixture over the opened out breast half. Fold over and secure by threading a bamboo skewer or toothpick through the cut edges of each breast. Repeat with the remaining chicken breast halves and herbed mixture.
- Heat the oil in an oven-proof heavy skillet or cast-iron ridged grill pan. Add the chicken skin-side down and cook over medium heat until lightly golden, 5 minutes. Turn the chicken skin side up. Sprinkle with salt and pepper.
- Place the pan in the oven. Roast the chicken until cooked through, about 10 minutes. Serve hot on warmed plates with Parsley Smashed Potatoes (see page 94) and Slow-Roast Tomatoes (see page 100).

**WHICH HERBS?**

Vary the fresh herb according to what is available. Choose any one or a combination of parsley, basil, chives, thyme, scallions, oregano, tarragon, watercress or arugula.

# French Leek Tart

- Preheat the oven to 350°F (180°C).
- Place a baking sheet in the oven to preheat.
- Melt the butter in a large skillet over a medium low heat. Add the leeks and cook, stirring frequently, until very soft and wilted, 20-30 minutes. Leave to cool slightly.
- Beat the eggs, crème fraîche or cream, salt, pepper and nutmeg until well combined. Add the cooled leeks to the egg mixture. Spread mixture over the pre-baked pastry shell. Place tart in the oven on the preheated baking sheet.
- Bake until the tart is golden and just set, 30 minutes. Leave to cool on a wire rack for 10 minutes before serving. Cut into wedges and serve hot, warm or at room temperature.

### VARIATIONS

## Onion Tart

Replace leeks with 4 large or 6 medium onions, finely sliced. Cook as directed for leeks. Add to the egg mixture and proceed as directed.

## Spinach Tart

Replace leeks with 2lb (1kg) spinach. Rinse spinach. Place in a large pan with the water still clinging to the leaves. Cook over high heat, stirring frequently, until wilted and bright green, 3-5 minutes. Drain and rinse in cold water. With your hands, squeeze spinach to remove excess water. Chop coarsely. Add to the egg mixture with 1 cup grated parmesan, gruyère or cheddar cheese. Proceed as directed.

## Broccoli Tart

Replace leeks with 1lb (500g) broccoli, stems finely sliced and florets separated. Steam over boiling, salted water until the stems are tender, 12-15 minutes. Leave to cool. Add the broccoli and 1 cup grated parmesan or cheddar cheese to the egg mixture and proceed as directed.

## Mushroom Tart

Replace leeks with 1 lb (500g) sliced brown or portabella mushrooms and 1 finely chopped onion. Heat 2 tbsp oil in a heavy skillet. Add the mushrooms and onion and cook, stirring constantly over high heat, until wilted and starting to crisp, 5 minutes. Remove from the pan and leave to cool. Add to the egg mixture and proceed as directed.

**SERVES 4-6**
FOR THE FILLING
4 tbsp butter
4 large leeks, finely sliced
2 eggs, beaten
1 cup crème fraîche or heavy cream
1 tsp salt
½ tsp black pepper
¼ tsp grated nutmeg
1 - 10in (25cm) pastry shell, pre-baked (see page 66)

**COOK'S TIP**
You can bake the tart up to 1 day in advance. Wrap in plastic wrap and refrigerate. For optimum flavor and texture, warm through in a 300°F (150°C) oven for 15 minutes before serving.

**HEALTH BITE**
If you are feeling calorie-conscious, replace ½ cup crème fraîche or heavy cream with milk or sour cream. For a more indulgent tart, replace the heavy cream or crème fraîche with mascarpone cheese.

# Perfect Pastry

**MAKES 1 - 10in (25cm) PASTRY SHELL**

1⅓ cups all-purpose flour
¼ tsp salt
6 tbsp chilled butter, cubed
1 egg yolk
2 tbsp cold water

**ESSENTIAL EQUIPMENT**

*1 - 10in (25cm) tart pan with a removable base*
*Baking beans (bought ceramic beans, or dried chickpeas)*

**COOK'S TIP**

You can make the pastry up to 2 days in advance. Wrap in plastic wrap and refrigerate, but be sure to return to room temperature before rolling out. Alternatively, line the tart with pastry up to 1 day in advance and refrigerate or freeze.

• Place the flour, salt and butter in a food processor; pulse until the mixture resembles fine crumbs. Add the egg yolk. Pulse until the pastry draws together, adding the water, ½ tbsp at a time, as needed. Turn out the pastry on to a lightly floured surface and knead briefly to make a smooth round.
• Alternatively, make the pastry by hand. Place the flour, salt and butter in a bowl. With 2 knives, cut the butter into the dry ingredients until the mixture resembles fine crumbs. Add the egg yolk and mix with a wooden spoon until the pastry draws together, adding the water, ½ tbsp at a time, as needed.
• Turn out the pastry on to a lightly floured surface and knead briefly to make a smooth round.
• On a lightly floured surface, roll out the pastry to a ⅛in (3mm) thickness. To line the tin, roll the pastry loosely around the rolling pin, then lift it and unroll carefully over the tart pan. Gently press the pastry over the base and up the sides of the pan. Use pastry scraps to patch any tears. Trim the edges of the pastry, letting it come up just above the sides of the pan. Chill or freeze for at least 15 minutes, to allow the pastry to relax in order to minimize shrinking.
• Preheat the oven to 400°F (200°C).
• Line the tart shell with baking parchment and fill with baking beans. Bake until the pastry is firm, 10 minutes. Remove the paper and beans. Continue baking until crisp and golden, 10 minutes. If not filling and baking immediately, leave to cool on a wire rack.

# Roast Cherry Tomato Spaghetti

- Preheat the oven to 400°F (200°C).
- In a roasting pan, combine the cherry tomatoes, garlic, red pepper flakes, oil and vinegar. Sprinkle with salt and pepper. Toss well to coat. Roast until soft and wilted, 20 minutes.
- Cook the pasta in a large pot of boiling, salted water until firm to the bite. Drain well and return pasta to the warm pot with the roast tomato sauce and basil, if using. Toss well to coat. Serve hot on warmed plates.

### VARIATION
## Roast Cherry Tomato Spaghetti with Goat Cheese
Cook the tomatoes and pasta as directed. Toss 4oz (125g) crumbled fresh creamy goat cheese together with the pasta and the sauce.

# Slow-Simmered Tomato Pasta Sauce

- Place the tomatoes, garlic and oil in a deep skillet over medium heat. Bring to a boil. Adjust the heat and simmer slowly, stirring occasionally, until thick, 30 minutes. Add salt and pepper to taste.
- Cook the pasta in a large pot of boiling, salted water until firm to the bite. Drain well and add pasta to the hot sauce. Toss well to coat. Serve hot on warmed plates, with parmesan.

### VARIATION
## Slow-Simmered Tomato Pasta Sauce with Molten Mozzarella
Cook tomatoes and pasta as directed. Add 4oz (125g) diced mozzarella to the pasta and the sauce.

**SERVES 4**
1lb (500g) cherry tomatoes
1 garlic clove, crushed
¼ tsp red pepper flakes
¼ cup extra virgin olive oil
1 tbsp balsamic vinegar
salt, black pepper
1lb (500g) spaghetti
1 handful fresh basil leaves, optional

**COOK'S TIP**
If you can't find cherry tomatoes, use 8 fresh ripe tomatoes cut into equal sized chunks.

**HEALTH BITE**
Pasta is great food for keeping our motors running. Its slow release of carbohydrates can keep energy levels high for hours.

**SERVES 4**
2 - 14oz (400g) cans italian plum tomatoes, chopped
6 garlic cloves, crushed
6 tbsp extra virgin olive oil
salt, black pepper
1lb (500g) penne
freshly grated parmesan

**COOK'S TIP**
Make the sauce up to 3 days in advance. Cover and refrigerate.

**HEALTH BITE**
Tomatoes are an excellent source of lycopene, an antioxidant that has been shown to help reduce the risk of certain types of cancer. Recent research has shown that canned tomatoes contain even higher levels of lycopene than fresh tomatoes.

# Coriander Roast Lamb with Spiced Chickpea Sauce

• Place the coriander, cumin, allspice, cinnamon, onion, garlic, tomato, lemon juice and oil in a food processor; pulse to a smooth paste.

• Use a small, sharp knife to cut small slits in the lamb. Push some of the coriander mixture into the slits. Rub the lamb all over with the remaining coriander mixture. Marinate for up to 1 hour at room temperature, or up to 4 hours in the refrigerator.

• Preheat the oven to 400°F (200°C).

• Rub the lamb all over with salt and pepper. Place in a roasting pan. Roast until medium rare, about 1 hour. Cover loosely with foil and leave to rest for 10 minutes before carving.

• While the lamb is roasting, make the spiced chickpea sauce. Place chickpeas, garlic, cumin, tabasco sauce, lemon, tahini, water and yogurt in a food processor; pulse until smooth. Add salt and pepper to taste.

• Carve lamb and serve hot on warmed plates with the spiced chickpea sauce.

## VARIATION
### Balsamic Roast Lamb with Garlic and Rosemary

Omit the coriander mixture. Replace with 6 crushed garlic cloves, 1 tbsp finely chopped fresh rosemary, 2 tbsp balsamic vinegar and 2 tbsp olive oil. Mix garlic, rosemary, vinegar and oil to a paste. Proceed as directed.

Omit Spiced Chickpea Sauce. Serve with Marinated White Beans with Olive Oil, Lemon and Chili (see page 101).

---

**SERVES 4 - 6**

1½ tsp ground coriander
½ tsp ground cumin
¼ tsp ground allspice
¼ tsp ground cinnamon
1 onion, chopped
4 garlic cloves, chopped
1 ripe tomato
2 tbsp lemon juice
2 tbsp olive oil
1 leg of lamb, weighing about 4¼ lb (2kg)
2 tsp salt, 1 tsp black pepper

FOR THE SPICED CHICKPEA SAUCE

14oz (400g) can chickpeas, drained and rinsed
2 garlic cloves, crushed
½ tsp ground cumin
¼ tsp tabasco sauce
2 tbsp lemon juice
5 tbsp tahini
5 tbsp water
½ cup greek-style whole milk yogurt or sour cream
salt, black pepper

**COOK'S TIP**

Lamb takes about 15 minutes per 1lb (500g) to roast to medium rare at 400°F (200°C), so, if your leg of lamb weighs any more or less than 4¼ lb (2kg), calculate the cooking time accordingly.

## SERVES

- 4 pork chops, about 1in (2.5cm) thick
- 1 tbsp sunflower oil
- 2 tbsp butter
- 2 apples, cut into 8 wedges
- 4 shallots, halved but still attached at the root end
- 1 garlic clove, crushed
- ½ cup calvados
- salt, black pepper

**COOK'S TIP**

Calvados is a dry apple brandy produced in the Normandy region of northern France. Pork and calvados are traditional culinary partners, and complement each other perfectly.

# Pan-Fried Pork Chops with Golden Shallots and Calvados Sauce

• Trim off excess fat from the chops. With scissors, cut snips through the remaining fat at 1½in (4cm) intervals.

• Heat the oil in a large skillet over high heat. Add the chops to the pan and cook until golden brown, 2 minutes per side. Reduce heat to low, cover the pan and cook until there is no trace of pink near the bone but the pork is still moist and juicy, about 5 minutes per side. Remove the chops from the pan to a warmed dish. Cover with foil and keep warm in a 250°F (120°C) oven while you make the sauce.

• Turn the heat to medium high and allow the pan juices to reduce and caramelize, 2 minutes. Add the butter to the pan. Add the apples and shallots and cook, stirring occasionally, until soft and golden brown, 8 minutes. Add the garlic and calvados and bring to a boil. Cook, stirring and scraping the bottom of the pan, until reduced by half, 3-5 minutes. Add salt and pepper to taste.

• Arrange the chops on warmed plates and sprinkle with salt and pepper. Arrange shallots and apples on top and spoon over pan juices. Serve hot with Mustard Smashed Potatoes (see page 94).

# Olive Oil Braised Mediterranean Vegetables

**SERVES 4 AS A MAIN**

¼ cup extra virgin olive oil

1 medium onion, finely chopped

2 celery stalks, finely chopped

1 medium carrot, finely chopped

4 garlic cloves, crushed

½ tsp crumbled dried rosemary or 1 tsp finely chopped fresh rosemary

½ tsp red pepper flakes

1 medium eggplant, cut into ½ in (1cm) cubes

2 medium zucchini, cut into ½ in (1cm) cubes

2 red bell peppers, cored, seeded and cut into ½ in (1cm) cubes

2 potatoes, cut into ½ in (1cm) cubes

4 ripe fresh tomatoes or canned plum tomatoes, quartered

½ cup water

14oz (400g) can white beans, drained and rinsed

1 handful fresh basil, mint or parsley or a combination, chopped

salt, black pepper

additional extra virgin olive oil to serve

• Heat the oil in a large pot. Add the onion, celery, carrot and garlic and cook over medium heat, stirring constantly, until soft, 5 minutes. Add the rosemary, red pepper flakes, eggplant, zucchini, peppers, potato, tomatoes and water. Turn the heat down to low and cover. Cook gently, stirring occasionally, until very soft, 30 minutes.

• Stir in the beans and cook until hot through, 5 minutes. Add the herbs and salt and pepper to taste. Serve hot in warmed bowls, drizzled with olive oil.

**VARIATION**

## Olive Oil Braised Winter Vegetables

Replace eggplant, zucchini and red bell pepper with 1½ lb (750g) squash, cut into chunks, 2 leeks, thickly sliced, and 2 fennel bulbs, roughly chopped. Proceed as directed.

# Perfect Roast Chicken with Green Olives and Lemon Roast Potatoes

- Preheat the oven to 400°F (200°C).
- Smear the chicken all over with oil and rub with salt. Put a pinch each of salt and pepper inside the cavity, together with the olives.
- Combine the potato quarters with the garlic, lemon juice, oil, rosemary, salt and pepper. Mix well to coat each potato quarter evenly. Choose a roasting pan that will just accommodate the chicken and the vegetables. Place the chicken in the pan and surround with the potatoes.
- Roast the chicken for 1½ hours, basting every 20 minutes, until golden brown with a crisp skin. To test for doneness, stick a fork into the chicken under the wing and hold up the chicken, cavity down. If the juices run clear, not pink, it is cooked through. Remove from the oven and leave to rest for 10 minutes to allow the juices to settle.
- Carve and serve hot with the warm green olives, crisp garlicky potatoes and chicken juices.

**SERVES 4 - 6**
1 x 3lb (1.5kg) chicken
3 tbsp extra virgin olive oil
2 tsp salt
black pepper
5oz (150g) green olives

FOR THE POTATOES
2lb (1kg) potatoes,
 quartered lengthwise
2 garlic cloves, crushed
juice of 1 lemon
3 tbsp extra virgin olive oil
2 tsp finely chopped fresh
 rosemary or ½ tsp crumbled
 dried rosemary
1 tsp kosher salt
½ tsp black pepper

**COOK'S TIP**
This roast chicken carcass will make a wonderful stock. Place the bones in a pan and add cold water to cover. Bring to a boil, reduce heat and simmer for at least 1½ hours, adding water if necessary to keep the bones covered. Strain stock into a large bowl and refrigerate. Once the stock has chilled, you can remove the solidified layer of fat from the top.

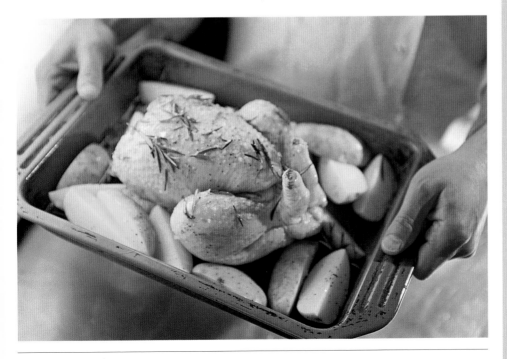

**SERVES 4 - 6**

2lb (1kg) piece beef suitable for stewing, braising or pot-roasting, such as a rump roast or or brisket

2 tsp black pepper

2 garlic cloves, finely chopped

1 onion, finely chopped

4 bacon slices, finely chopped

½ tsp dried thyme or 1 tsp fresh thyme

4 carrots, cut into 3in (8cm) lengths

4 celery stalks, cut into 3in (8cm) lengths

8 shallots or 2 onions, root end intact, peeled and quartered

8 whole garlic cloves

12 brown or portabella mushrooms

8 medium potatoes, halved lengthwise

1 cup red wine

2 tbsp cognac or brandy, optional

salt, black pepper

**COOK'S TIP**

This recipe is the ultimate in hands-off cooking. You don't even have to brown the meat and vegetables. Just place everything in the pot and cook very slowly while you get on with something else.

**HEALTH BITE**

Research shows that red wine in moderation may lower the risk of heart disease. Now that's news to drink to!

# Slow-Simmered Beef Daube with Red Wine and Garlic

• Preheat the oven to 300°F (150°C).

• Sprinkle the beef all over with black pepper. In a heavy-based pot, place the garlic, onion, bacon and thyme. Place the beef on top and surround with the carrots, celery, shallots or onions, garlic, mushrooms and potatoes. Pour over the red wine and cognac, if using. Place the pot over medium heat and bring just to a simmer. Cover and put into the oven to cook slowly until very tender, 3-4 hours, making sure that the liquid does not boil. Add salt and pepper to taste.

• Cut the beef into thick slices and place on warmed plates. Surround with the vegetables and spoon over the beef juices. Serve hot.

**VARIATION**

## Slow-Simmered Beef Stew with Red Wine and Garlic

Use stewing beef cut into 1½in (4cm) cubes in place of the whole piece of beef. Heat 1 tbsp olive oil in the cooking pot and fry meat a few pieces at a time until browned all over, 3 minutes. Remove from pot and proceed as directed.

# Best Sausages with Golden Onions, Red Peppers and Tomatoes

**SERVES 4**
8 italian sausages, pricked
2 onions, finely sliced
2 red bell peppers, cored, seeded and cut into fine strips
14oz (400g) can italian plum tomatoes, chopped
salt, black pepper
1 handful chopped fresh parsley, optional

• Heat a large skillet over medium heat. Add the sausages and cook until browned all over, 8-10 minutes. Remove from the pan and set aside.
• Add the onions to the pan, cover with a lid, and cook until soft and wilted, 5 minutes. Remove the cover and stir in the pepper strips. Cook, stirring frequently, until the onion is golden and the pepper tender, 10 minutes. Add the tomatoes and cook, stirring occasionally, until thickened, 10 minutes.
• Turn the heat to low and return the sausages to the pan. Cook, stirring occasionally, for a further 10 minutes. Add salt and pepper to taste. Serve hot on warmed plates, sprinkled with parsley, if using.

**VARIATION**
## Best Sausages with Golden Onions, Cabbage & Tomatoes
Omit red bell peppers. Replace with ½ savoy or white cabbage, cored and shredded. Cook as directed.

## SERVES 4

8 lamb rib or loin chops
2 garlic cloves, crushed
2 tsp black pepper
½ tsp dried thyme or
1 tsp fresh thyme leaves
1 tbsp balsamic vinegar
1 tbsp extra virgin olive oil
salt
lemon wedges

## SERVES 4 AS A MAIN, 6 AS A SIDE

FOR THE DHAL
2 tbsp butter
1 onion, finely chopped
1 garlic clove, finely chopped
1 tbsp freshly grated ginger
8oz (250g) red lentils
½ tsp turmeric
3 cups water
salt

FOR THE AROMATICS
2 tbsp butter
½ tsp red pepper flakes
3 bay leaves
½ tsp cumin seeds
½ tsp fennel seeds
2 garlic cloves, finely
    chopped

### COOK'S TIP
You can cook the dhal up to 1 day in advance. Cover and refrigerate. However, for fullest flavor, add the sizzling and fragrant aromatics to the hot dhal just before serving.

### HEALTH BITE
High fiber and low in fat, lentils are also an excellent source of protein, especially when eaten with rice. Rice and lentils combined make up all 8 essential amino acids, so this traditional Indian staple of rice with dhal is the perfect protein provider.

# Pan-Grilled Balsamic Lamb Chops

• Rub the chops with garlic, pepper and thyme. Drizzle over the vinegar and oil. Marinate, turning occasionally, for up to 1 hour at room temperature or up to 4 hours in the refrigerator.
• Preheat a cast-iron ridged grill pan or outdoor grill. Grill or broil the chops until medium rare, 3 minutes per side. Sprinkle with salt. Serve hot on warmed plates with lemon wedges and Sizzling Garlic Greens (see page 93).

# Red Lentil Dhal with Aromatics

• For the dhal, melt the butter in a pan over a medium high heat. Add the onion, garlic and ginger and cook, stirring constantly, until fragrant, 1-2 minutes. Add the lentils, turmeric and water and bring to a boil. Turn down the heat and simmer, stirring occasionally, until thickened slightly, 20 - 30 minutes. Add salt to taste.
• For the aromatics, melt the butter in a small skillet over medium high heat. Add the red pepper flakes, bay, cumin, fennel and garlic and cook until the garlic is golden, 30-60 seconds. Stir into the dhal and serve immediately with steamed rice.

# Moroccan Chicken Stew with Saffron and Apricot

**SERVES 4**

4 tbsp butter
2 onions, finely chopped
4 garlic cloves, crushed
pinch saffron threads
1 tbsp turmeric
1½ tsp ground cumin
1½ tsp ground coriander
1½ tsp paprika
1 tsp black pepper
¼ tsp cayenne pepper
8 chicken thighs, skinned
juice of 1 lemon
1 cup chicken stock or water
4oz (125g) dried apricots
14oz (400g) can chickpeas, drained
salt

• Melt the butter in a heavy-based pan over medium low heat. Add the onions, garlic, saffron, turmeric, cumin, coriander, paprika, pepper and cayenne and cook, stirring occasionally, until onions are very soft, 10 minutes.
• Add the chicken, lemon juice, stock, apricots and chickpeas and bring just to simmering point. Cook gently until the chicken is tender and opaque throughout, with no trace of pink at the bone, 30-40 minutes. Add salt to taste.
• Arrange the chicken pieces on warmed plates and spoon over the sauce. Scatter with add-ons, if using. Serve hot, with buttered couscous or warm flatbread.

**COOK'S TIP**
The stew can be made up to 1 day in advance. Cover and refrigerate.

## MOROCCAN CHICKEN STEW ADD-ONS
Add a final flourish of color, texture and flavor to this sweetly spiced stew with 1 handful cilantro or parsley or mint leaves and 2 tbsp slivered almonds.

## VARIATION
### Moroccan Lamb Stew with Saffron and Apricot
Replace chicken with 2lb (1kg) cubed stewing lamb, such as shoulder. Omit lemon juice and replace with the juice of 1 orange. Proceed as directed, but cover the pan tightly and cook very gently, taking care not to let the liquid boil. Cook until the lamb is very tender, 2-3 hours. Serve as directed.

**SERVES 4**

FOR THE LEMON MUSTARD VINAIGRETTE

1 tsp dijon-style mustard

2 tbsp lemon juice

⅓ cup extra virgin olive oil

salt, black pepper

4 x 6oz (175g) fish
  fillets (see below)

1 tbsp extra virgin olive oil

**WHY ORGANIC?**

Organic farmed fish is given natural feeds only and is farmed in a way that minimizes harm to the environment. The fish can swim freely and do not undergo routine medication.

# Grilled Fish with Lemon Mustard Vinaigrette

• Preheat a broiler to as hot as possible, allowing 15 minutes.

• For the dressing, combine mustard, lemon and oil in a small pan. Add salt and pepper to taste. Place over a low heat and warm through until tepid. 1-2 minutes.

• Place the fish skin-side up on an oiled oven tray. Broil, without turning, until cooked through (see below). Sprinkle with salt and pepper. Serve on warmed plates with the warmed dressing spooned over.

**WHICH FISH?**

Broil thin fish fillets about ½in (1cm) thick, such as sole, trout, mullet, red snapper, flounder or sea bass until just opaque throughout, 3-5 minutes.

Broil thick fish fillets about 1in (2.5cm) thick, such as cod, swordfish or turbot until just opaque throughout, 8-10 minutes.

Broil salmon fillets until the flesh turns opaque but is still moist and pink in the middle, 6-8 minutes.

**VARIATIONS**

## Grilled Fish with Lemon Tomato Vinaigrette

Make vinaigrette as directed, adding 1 finely seeded and diced tomato.

## Grilled Fish with Lemon Herb Vinaigrette

Make vinaigrette as directed, adding 1 tsp finely chopped fresh thyme, tarragon, parsley, fennel, dill or oregano.

## Grilled Fish with Lemon Caper Vinaigrette

Make vinaigrette as directed, adding 1 tbsp drained and rinsed capers.

**SERVES 4**

1 tbsp olive oil

2 garlic cloves, crushed

4 shallots, finely chopped

7oz (200g) wild mushrooms, chopped

4 x 8oz (250g) sirloin steaks, 1in (2.5cm) thick

½ cup red wine

1 tsp butter

salt, black pepper

# Wine-Glazed Steak with Mushrooms

• Heat the oil in a heavy skillet. Add the garlic, shallots and mushrooms and cook, stirring constantly, over high heat, until wilted and starting to crisp, 5 minutes. Remove from the pan and reserve.

• Add the steaks to the hot pan. Cook for 3 minutes per side for rare, 4 minutes per side for medium rare, 6 minutes per side for well done. Remove to warmed plates to rest.

• Add the wine to the hot pan. Boil until reduced by half, 2 minutes. Return the mushrooms to the pan. Heat through, stirring constantly, 1 minute. Remove from heat and stir in butter. Spoon mushrooms and wine juices over the steaks. Sprinkle with salt and pepper. Serve immediately.

**VARIATION**

## Wine-Glazed Fillet Steak

Replace sirloin steaks with 6oz (175g) fillet steaks, 2in (5cm) thick. Cook as directed, for 3 minutes per side for rare, 4 minutes per side for medium rare, 6 minutes per side for well done.

# Eat Your
# Greens

**SERVES 4 AS A MAIN, 6 AS A SIDE**

¼ cup extra virgin olive oil
1 onion, finely sliced
4 garlic cloves, finely sliced
¼ tsp red pepper flakes
3 red bell peppers, cored,
  seeded and cut into strips
  2in (5cm) long and 1in
  (2.5cm) wide
4 medium potatoes, cut into
  2in (5cm) chunks
14oz (400g) can italian plum
  tomatoes, chopped
5oz (150g) pitted black olives
1 handful fresh basil or
  parsley, chopped

**SERVES 4 AS A SIDE**

2 tbsp extra virgin olive oil
2 garlic cloves, finely sliced
¼ tsp red pepper flakes
10oz–1lb (300 - 500g)
  greens (see opposite)
2 tsp red wine vinegar or
  lemon juice
salt, black pepper

**HEALTH BITE**
Vitamin rich and calcium packed, dark leafy greens are super-charged with anti-carcinogenic antioxidants.

# Red Peppers stewed with Potatoes and Olives

• Heat the oil in a heavy based pot. Add the onion and cook, stirring frequently, over medium heat until soft and just golden, 5 minutes.
• Add the garlic, red pepper flakes, pepper, potato, tomatoes and olives. Turn the heat to low and simmer gently, stirring occasionally, until the potatoes are tender, 30-40 minutes. Stir in the basil or parsley. Add salt and pepper to taste. Serve hot or at room temperature.

# Sizzling Garlic Greens

• Heat the oil in a large frying pan. Add the garlic and red pepper flakes and cook over medium high heat until the garlic is just golden, 1 minute.
• Add the greens and cook, stirring occasionally, until wilted and tender but still bright green (see below). Add the vinegar or lemon juice and salt and pepper to taste. Serve hot.

**WHICH GREENS?**
Any greens work for this recipe, but the cooking time will vary. Choose from:

1lb (500g) spinach or swiss chard, washed, stems finely chopped and leaves coarsely chopped. Cook for 5-8 minutes.
1lb (500g) cabbage, core cut out and discarded, leaves coarsely shredded. Cook for 15-20 minutes.
1lb (500g) broccoli rabe, stems finely sliced, florets separated. Steam over boiling, salted water until the stems are just tender, 6-8 minutes. Add to garlic and chilli flakes in pan as directed. Cook for 5-7 minutes.
10oz (300g) kale, coarsely chopped. Cook for 15-20 minutes.
10oz (300g) spring greens, coarsely chopped. Cook for 15-20 minutes.

# Smashed Potatoes

**SERVES 4 AS A SIDE**

2lb (1kg) potatoes, cut into equal-sized chunks

2 garlic cloves

¾ cup milk, sour cream, heavy cream, crème fraîche or reserved potato cooking water

¼ cup olive oil or 4 tbsp butter

salt, black pepper, nutmeg

**HEALTH BITE**

Leaving the skin on the potatoes adds extra nutrition and an earthy flavor to smashed potatoes. It's up to you how calorific you make your smash. Your options range from fat-free but nutritionally enhanced potato water to richly indulgent crème fraîche.

- Place the potato chunks and garlic in a pot of salted water to cover. Bring to a boil. Adjust the heat and simmer until soft, 20-30 minutes. Drain, reserving the potato water, if using.
- Return the potatoes to the dry pot. Return pot to a very low heat. Smash potatoes with a wooden spoon, beating in milk, sour cream, heavy cream, crème fraîche or cooking water. Beat in olive oil or butter. Add salt, pepper and nutmeg to taste. Serve immediately.

**VARIATIONS**

## Horseradish Smashed Potatoes

Add 2 tbsp horseradish sauce to the smashed potatoes. Mix until combined.

## Goat Cheese Smashed Potatoes

Add 4oz (125g) crumbled goat cheese to the smashed potatoes. Mix until combined.

## Parsley Smashed Potatoes

Add 1 handful coarsely chopped parsley to the smashed potatoes. Mix until combined.

## Mustard Smashed Potatoes

Add 2 tbsp creamy and 2 tbsp grainy dijon-style mustard to the smashed potatoes. Mix until combined.

## Carrot Smashed Potatoes

Add 2 grated carrots to the smashed potatoes. Mix until combined.

## Pesto Smashed Potatoes

Add 4 tbsp pesto to the smashed potatoes. Mix until combined.

## Smashed Winter Roots

Replace half the potatoes with celery root, parsnips, rutabaga or turnips, or a combination, cut into equal-sized chunks. Cook as directed.

# Roast Winter Squash

• Preheat oven to 400°F (200°C).
• Combine the garlic and oil. Cut the squash in half lengthwise and scoop out the seeds. Brush the flesh with the garlic oil. Sprinkle with salt and pepper. Place cut side down on a baking sheet.
• Roast until the skin is wrinkled and the flesh is very soft, about 1 hour. If necessary, cut into portions. Serve hot, cut side up, with salt, pepper and olive oil or butter. Alternatively, use to make Roast Winter Squash Mash (see below).

## VARIATIONS

### Roast Winter Squash Mash with Ginger

Roast the squash as directed. Scrape away the flesh from the skin and place in a food processor with 2 tbsp butter and 1 tbsp grated fresh ginger; purée until smooth. Add salt and pepper to taste. Serve hot.

### Roast Winter Squash Mash with Crème Fraîche and Cheese

Roast the squash as directed. Scrape away the flesh from the skin and place in a food processor with 2 tbsp butter, 4 tbsp grated parmesan or cheddar and 2 tbsp crème fraîche; purée until smooth. Add salt, pepper and nutmeg to taste. Serve hot.

**SERVES 4 AS A SIDE**
1 garlic clove, crushed
1 tbsp extra virgin olive oil
3lb (1.5kg) butternut or acorn squash (about 1 large or 2 small squash)
salt, black pepper
olive oil or butter to serve

**COOK'S TIP**
Squashes differ in size and shape but they nearly all have bright orange or yellow flesh and a sweet, earthy flavor, both intensified by oven-roasting.
When roasted, winter squash makes a richly colored and flavored side dish for grilled or roast meats. For a vegetarian main meal, choose smaller squashes and serve one half per person, with plenty of butter, grated cheese and a scraping of nutmeg.

**HEALTH BITE**
Squash is chock-full of nutrients, low in calories, high in Vitamin A and potassium, and is one of the easiest vegetables to digest.

**SERVES 4**

1lb (500g) raw beet
¾ cup heavy cream
4oz (125g) gruyère or
  cheddar cheese, grated
salt, black pepper

**COOK'S TIP**

Cut off the leaves from raw beets
when cooking, but do not peel or
trim root ends as this releases all
the color into the water.
Alternatively, use pre-cooked
beets.

# Creamy Beet Gratin

• To cook beets, place whole in boiling water. Simmer until tender when pierced with the tip of a knife, 35-45 minutes, depending on size. Leave to cool. Peel and cut into ¼ in (5mm) slices.
• Preheat oven to 400°F (200°C).
• Layer the beet slices in a buttered baking dish. Pour over the cream and sprinkle with cheese, salt and pepper.
• Bake until the topping is golden and just crisp, 15-20 minutes.

VARIATIONS
## Creamy Parsnip Gratin

Omit beets and replace with 1½ lb (750g) medium parsnips, cut into ¼ in (5mm) slices. Cook in boiling water until tender when pierced with the tip of a knife, 5-8 minutes. Drain well and proceed as directed.

## Creamy Potato Gratin

Omit beets and replace with 1½ lb (750g) potatoes, cut into ¼ in (5mm) slices. Cook in boiling water until tender when pierced with the tip of a knife, 5-8 minutes. Drain well and proceed as directed.

## Creamy Turnip Gratin

Omit beets and replace with 1½ lb (750g) medium turnips, cut into ¼ in (5mm) slices. Cook in boiling water until tender when pierced with the tip of a knife, 5-8 minutes. Drain well and proceed as directed.

# Slow **Roast** Tomatoes

**SERVES 4 AS A SIDE**

6 ripe tomatoes, halved
2 garlic cloves
salt, black pepper
1 tbsp balsamic vinegar
2 tbsp extra virgin olive oil
additional extra virgin olive oil
  for serving
1 handful fresh herbs,
  chopped, such as parsley,
  basil, marjoram or a
  combination

**COOK'S TIP**

When cooking with fresh tomatoes outside peak season, it is well worth thinking ahead and buying the tomatoes a few days in advance of using. Set them on a tray, making sure they are not touching, by the kitchen window. Never store tomatoes in the refrigerator, as refrigeration spoils their texture and aroma.

• Preheat the oven to 250°F (120°C).
• Place the tomatoes on an oven tray, cut side up. Cut garlic clove in half and cut each half into 3 slivers. Lay a sliver of garlic onto each tomato half. Sprinkle each tomato half with a pinch of salt and pepper. Drizzle over the vinegar and oil. Slow roast until very soft and wilted, 2 hours.
• Serve hot or at room temperature, drizzled with additional olive oil and scattered with fresh herbs.

# Marinated Beans with Olive Oil, Lemon and Chili

• For the dressing, combine the garlic, lemon juice, oil and red pepper flakes. Add salt and pepper to taste.

• Place the beans in a pan of water to cover. Bring just to the boil. Drain immediately and combine the hot beans with the dressing. Toss gently to coat. Add the tomatoes and the herbs. Add salt and pepper to taste. Serve warm with grilled meats or fish, or at room temperature with green salad leaves.

### WHICH BEANS?

white beans, cannellini, flageolet, lima beans or chick-peas all work well with this recipe.

**SERVES 4**

2 garlic cloves, crushed
2 tbsp lemon juice
⅓ cup extra virgin olive oil
¼ tsp red pepper flakes
salt, black pepper
2 - 14oz (400g) cans beans
  (see below), drained and
  rinsed
4 ripe tomatoes, diced
1 handful fresh parsley or
  basil, coarsely chopped

### COOK'S TIP

If you are using dried beans, you will need 8oz (250g). Soak overnight in water to cover. Drain, rinse and cook in water to cover until tender, 1-1½ hours. Be sure to combine with the dressing while still hot.

### HEALTH BITE

Dried beans and pulses are now recognised as one of nature's healthiest foods - low in fat, high in fiber, rich in iron, phosphorous and B vitamins. As well as being a good source of protein, their high carbohydrate content delivers a gradual release of energy.

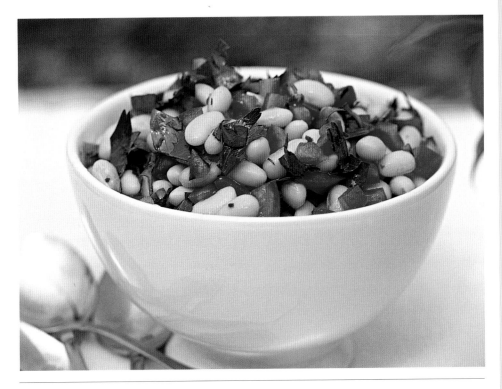

**SERVES 4 AS A SIDE**

2½ lb (1.25kg) mixed root
    vegetables (see opposite)
1 head garlic, separated into
    cloves but unpeeled
½ tsp crumbled dried
    rosemary or 1 tsp finely
    chopped fresh rosemary
½ tbsp balsamic vinegar
¼ cup extra virgin olive oil
kosher salt, black pepper

**HEALTH BITE**

Leave skins on root vegetables
where possible, as the skin and the
flesh just beneath the skin are valuable nutritionally, containing the
most fiber and vitamin C.

# Roast Winter Roots

• Preheat the oven to 400°F (200°C).
• Place the vegetables and garlic in a single layer in a roasting dish. Sprinkle with rosemary, vinegar, oil, salt and pepper. Toss well to coat. Roast until golden and tender, 40 minutes - 1 hour.

**WHICH ROOTS?**

Any roots or combination of roots will work for this recipe. To minimize differences in cooking times, you will need to cut the fast-cooking vegetables into slightly larger pieces than the slow-cookers. Choose from:

potatoes, quartered
carrots, halved lengthwise
medium parsnips, quartered lengthwise
celery root, peeled and cut into wedges
turnips, quartered
sweet potatoes, quartered
beets, quartered
shallots, whole and peeled
onions, peeled and quartered but still attached by the root end
rutabaga, peeled and cut into wedges
jerusalem artichokes, halved

# Spring Vegetable Ragoût

**SERVES 4 AS A MAIN, 6 AS A SIDE**

2 tbsp extra virgin olive oil
1½ lb (750g) mixed spring
vegetables (see opposite)
lemon wedges
⅔ cup boiling vegetable
stock or water
2 tsp butter
2 tbsp lemon juice
salt, black pepper
1 handful fresh herbs, torn
or roughly chopped
(see opposite)

• Heat the oil in a large skillet. Add the vegetables and cook, stirring constantly, over medium heat until just starting to soften, 5 minutes. Add the boiling stock or water and simmer until the vegetables are crisp-tender, 10 minutes.

• Remove from heat and add butter and lemon juice. Add salt and pepper to taste. Ladle into warmed bowls, scatter with fresh herbs and serve hot.

**WHICH VEGETABLES?**

Any combination of tender spring vegetables will work for this recipe. To minimize differences in cooking times, you need to cut the fast cooking vegetables into slightly larger pieces than the slow cooking ones. Choose from:

asparagus, cut into 3in (7.5cm) lengths
radishes, halved
button mushrooms, whole
scallions, cut into 3in (7.5cm) lengths
cherry tomatoes, whole
carrots, cut into sticks 3 x ½in (7.5 x 1cm)
fava beans, shelled
peas, shelled
fennel, halved and sliced ½in (1cm) thick
snow peas, whole
zucchini, cut into sticks ½in (1cm) thick and 2in (7.5cm) long
green beans, whole
spring turnips, cut into 3 x ½in (7.5 x 1cm) sticks
celery, cut into 3 x ½in (7.5 x 1cm) sticks
cauliflower cut into tiny florets
broccoli rabe, leaves and stalks chopped and heads cut into tiny florets

**WHICH HERBS?**

Try any one or a combination of fresh herbs. Our preference is for the classic *fines herbes* quartet - chervil, chives, parsley and tarragon.

# **Best** Baked Potatoes

**SERVES 4**

4 x 8oz (250g) potatoes
salt, black pepper

TO SERVE

1 large knob of butter or
  1 tbsp olive oil per potato

• Arrange the oven rack in the centre of the oven. Place a baking sheet on the rack. Preheat the oven to 400°F (200°C).

• Pierce the potatoes a few times with a fork or skewer. Rinse the potatoes under cold running water. While they are still damp, sprinkle evenly with salt. Place the potatoes at least 4in (10cm) apart on to the hot baking sheet. Bake until crusty outside and soft inside, 1-1½ hours.

• To serve, cut a cross on the top of each potato. Push the ends together to open it up. Sprinkle with salt and pepper. Add butter or oil. Serve hot, as a side with roasts or stews, or make a meal of it served with a salad.

**COOK'S TIP**
Never bake potatoes either in the microwave or in the oven wrapped in plastic wrap or foil, or the potatoes will be steamed, not baked.

## VARIATION
## Best Baked Potato with Cherry Tomatoes

This is our favorite topping. Make the Roast Cherry Tomatoes on page 68. Cook and cut open the potatoes as directed. Top with greek-style whole milk yogurt or sour cream, then spoon over the tomatoes.

**BEST BAKED POTATO GO-WITHS**
Finish with any one or a combination of the following:
½ cup sour cream or whole milk greek-style yogurt
4oz (125g) grated cheese
2 tbsp finely chopped chives or scallions

# **Best** Baked
# Sweet Potato

**SERVES 4**

4 sweet potatoes
salt, pepper, nutmeg,
  cinnamon

TO SERVE

1 large knob of butter
  per potato

• Arrange the oven rack in the center of the oven. Preheat the oven to 400°F (200°C).

• Pierce the potatoes a few times with a fork or skewer. Place the potatoes at least 4in (10cm) apart in an oven tray. Bake until very soft, 1-1½ hours.

• To serve, cut a cross on the top of each potato. Push the ends together to open it up. Sprinkle with salt, pepper, nutmeg and cinnamon. Serve hot with butter.

**COOK'S TIP**
We recommend using a foil lined oven tray with sides, rather than a baking sheet, because sweet potatoes tend to leak syrupy juices as they bake.

# Dressings for Leafy Salads

## Honey Mustard

**EACH MAKES ENOUGH TO DRESS
4 HANDFULS SALAD LEAVES**
1 garlic clove, crushed
1 tbsp honey
1 tsp dijon-style mustard
2 tsp grainy dijon mustard
2 tbsp red wine vinegar
⅓ cup extra virgin olive oil
salt, black pepper

• Mix together garlic, honey, mustards, vinegar and olive oil until thick and smooth. Add salt and pepper to taste.

## Lemon Garlic

**SERVES 4**
1 garlic clove, crushed
2 tbsp lemon juice
⅓ cup extra virgin olive oil
salt, black pepper

• Mix together garlic, lemon and oil until smooth. Add salt and pepper to taste.

## Avocado Yogurt

**SERVES 4**
1 avocado
1 garlic clove, crushed
2 scallions, chopped
½ cup greek-style whole
   milk yogurt or sour cream
1 tbsp red wine vinegar
1 tbsp extra virgin olive oil
salt, black pepper

• Place avocado, garlic, scallion, yogurt or cream, vinegar and oil in a food processor; pulse until smooth. Add salt and pepper to taste.

## Creamy Shallot

**SERVES 4**
1 shallot, finely chopped
2 tbsp red wine vinegar
¼ cup extra virgin olive oil
¼ cup crème fraîche or sour
   cream
salt, black pepper

• Mix together the shallot, vinegar, oil and crème fraîche or sour cream until thick and smooth. Add salt and pepper to taste.

**COOK'S TIP**
You can make any of these dressings up to 1 day in advance. Cover and refrigerate. For the avocado dressing, be sure to press plastic wrap directly on the surface to keep from it turning brown.

# Balsamic Baked Onions

4 medium to large onions, red or yellow, peeled with root ends intact
2 tbsp extra virgin olive oil
2 tbsp balsamic vinegar
salt, black pepper

**HEALTH BITE**
Onions, like their relative garlic, are a good source of heart-protective antioxidants.

• Preheat the oven to 400°F (200°C).
• Cut a deep cross about 2in (5cm) deep in the top of each onion. Place the onions in a baking dish with a few tablespoons of water. Drizzle over oil and vinegar. Sprinkle with salt and pepper. Cover with foil and bake for 30 minutes. Remove the foil and bake until very tender and lightly crisp around the edges, 30 minutes.
• Spread the onions open. Serve hot, with add-ons (see below), if using.

**BALSAMIC BAKED ONIONS ADD-ONS**
Sprinkle over any or a combination of the following ingredients to transform these slow-cooked onions from side dish to main event:

1 cup crumbled blue cheese
½ cup sour cream
1 cup grated cheddar or gruyère cheese

# New Potato Salad with Shallot Vinaigrette

- Place the potato pieces in a large pan of cold water. Bring to a boil. Adjust heat and simmer gently until tender but still firm when pierced with the tip of a knife, 10-15 minutes. Drain.
- While the potatoes are cooking, make the vinaigrette. Mix shallots, vinegar and oil until combined.
- Add the hot potatoes to the vinaigrette with mix-ins, if using. Toss gently to coat each potato piece. Add salt and pepper to taste. Serve warm or at room temperature.

### VARIATION
## New Potato Salad with Crème Fraîche
Prepare the potatoes and vinaigrette as directed. Add ½ cup crème fraîche and mix gently to coat evenly.

### NEW POTATO SALAD MIX-INS
Vary the flavor and texture of this classic French-style potato salad by adding 2 tbsp finely chopped fresh herbs, such as dill, parsley or chives, 1 tbsp grainy dijon mustard or 2 celery stalks, finely chopped.

**SERVES 4 AS A SIDE**
1½ lb (750g) new potatoes, cut into bite-size pieces
2 shallots, finely chopped, or 4 scallions finely sliced
2 tbsp red wine vinegar
¼ cup extra virgin olive oil
salt, black pepper

**COOK'S TIP**
If serving the salad warm, you can cook and dress the potatoes up to 45 minutes in advance. If serving at room temperature, you can make the salad up to 1 day in advance. Cover and refrigerate, but, for optimum flavor, be sure to return to room temperature before serving.

# Something Sweet

# Upside **Down** Red Plum
## Caramel Cake

**SERVES 6-8**

FOR THE CARAMEL
¾ cup sugar
⅓ cup + 1 tbsp water
4 large red plums, halved

FOR THE CAKE
1 cup all-purpose flour
2 tsp baking powder
12 tbsp butter, softened
¾ cup granulated sugar
4 tbsp ground almonds
4 eggs, beaten
1 tsp vanilla extract

**ESSENTIAL EQUIPMENT**
*10in (25cm) cake pan, buttered*

**COOK'S TIP**
Caramel is basically burnt sugar.
There are just a few important
points to remember in order to
guarantee caramel success every
time. Once the syrup has boiled,
do not stir as this encourages
crystallization. If your caramel is
coloring too fast, prevent further
cooking by plunging the base of
the pan into cold water. If it sets
too hard to pour, return the pan to
a low heat and warm gently until
it melts.

- Preheat the oven to 300°F (150°C). Butter the cake pan.
- Place the sugar and water in a heavy-based saucepan over a low heat. Stir constantly with a wooden spoon to dissolve sugar. Do not allow the liquid to boil until the sugar has completely dissolved to form a clear syrup. Raise the heat to medium and bring the syrup to a boil. Boil rapidly until the syrup starts to turn brown around the edge of the pan. Lower the heat and continue to cook to a dark golden brown. Do not stir with a spoon, but swirl the pan once or twice so that the caramel colors evenly. Pour immediately into the buttered cake pan.
- Arrange the plums skin side up over the caramel.
- Sift the flour and baking powder into a large bowl. Add butter, sugar, almonds, eggs and vanilla. Beat until just smooth and evenly blended, 1-2 minutes. Spread the cake mixture over the fruit. Bake until the top is golden brown and the sides of the cake have pulled away from the pan, about 50 minutes.
- Leave to cool for 2-3 minutes, then run a knife around the sides of the cake and turn out onto a serving dish. If any pieces of fruit stick to the pan, use a spatula to remove and press back into place. Serve warm or at room temperature.

**VARIATIONS**

## Upside Down Strawberry Caramel Cake
Replace plums with 2lb (1kg) ripe strawberries. Proceed as directed.

## Upside Down Mango Caramel Cake
Replace plums with 3 medium, sliced mangoes. Proceed as directed.

## Upside Down Apple Caramel Cake
Replace plums with 4 quartered apples. Proceed as directed.

# Quick-Fix Toppings for Vanilla Ice Cream

## Toffee Bananas

**SERVES 4**

5 tbsp soft brown sugar
4 tbsp butter
6 tbsp heavy cream
vanilla ice cream
2 bananas, diagonally sliced

- Place the sugar, butter and cream in a small pan over medium heat and bring to the boil, stirring constantly.
- Have the ice cream ready in bowls. Top with banana slices. Drizzle over hot toffee sauce. Serve immediately.

## Very Berry

**SERVES 4**

2 cups blueberries,
  blackberries, raspberries,
  strawberries or
  a combination
2 tbsp sugar
vanilla ice cream

- Place the berries and sugar in a heavy pan over a low heat. Cook, stirring occasionally, until it is hot through and the juices start to run, about 10 minutes. Do not allow to boil.
- Have the ice cream ready in bowls. Spoon over hot berries and juices. Serve immediately.

## Chocolate Fudge

**SERVES 4**

½ cup heavy cream
1 tbsp dark brown sugar
2 tbsp butter
4oz (125g) dark chocolate,
  broken into pieces
1 tsp vanilla extract
vanilla ice cream

- Heat the cream, sugar and butter in a small pan until just simmering. Remove from the heat. Add the chocolate and vanilla and leave to stand for 1 minute. Stir until smooth and glossy.
- Have the ice cream ready in bowls. Drizzle over the hot sauce. Serve immediately.

## Caramelized Apples

**SERVES 4**

4 tbsp butter
4 tbsp light brown sugar
4 ripe firm apples, cored and
  cut into 8 pieces
¼ cup water
vanilla ice cream

- Melt the butter in a large skillet over medium heat. Add the sugar and stir to dissolve. Add the apples and cook, shaking the pan frequently, until the apples are golden brown, 5 minutes. Add the water and simmer until the apples are tender, 2 minutes.
- Have the ice cream ready in bowls. Top with hot apples and juices. Serve immediately.

# Peach-Ginger **Crisp** with Oatmeal

- Preheat the oven to 375°F (190°C).
- Place the peaches, sugar, lemon and ginger in an 8 x 10 x 2in (20 x 26 x 5cm) buttered baking dish and toss together gently to combine.
- For the topping, place the flour, oatmeal, salt, sugar and butter in a food processor; pulse until coarse and crumbly. Alternatively, mix the flour, oatmeal, salt and sugar in a bowl. Use 2 knives to cut the butter into the flour mixture until coarse and crumbly.
- Cover the fruit with the topping and bake until the topping is golden brown and the fruit is tender, 45 minutes. Serve hot.

**VARIATIONS**

## Apple-Cinnamon Crisp with Oatmeal

Replace peaches with 6 cored and sliced apples. Replace ginger with 1 tsp ground cinnamon. Proceed as directed.

## Strawberry-Rhubarb Crisp with Oatmeal

Replace peaches with 2lb (1kg) rhubarb cut into ½in (1cm) pieces and 8oz (250g) halved strawberries. Omit ginger and increase sugar to 1 cup. Proceed as directed.

## Nectarine-Raspberry Crisp with Oatmeal

Replace peaches with 4 nectarines sliced ½in (1cm) thick and 8oz (250g) raspberries. Omit ginger. Proceed as directed.

## Blueberry-Pear Crisp with Oatmeal

Replace peaches with 4 cored and sliced pears and 8oz (250g) blueberries. Omit ginger. Proceed as directed.

**SERVES 4-6**
6 peaches, sliced ½in (1cm) thick
2 tbsp sugar
1 tbsp lemon juice
2 tbsp grated fresh ginger

FOR THE TOPPING
¾ cup all-purpose flour
2oz (60g) oatmeal
¼ tsp salt
1 cup light brown sugar
1 x 4oz (125g) stick butter, chilled and cubed

**HEALTH BITE**
Oats are an excellent source of iron, magnesium and soluble fiber, and are low in saturated fat and sodium. Eaten regularly, oats may also help to lower cholesterol levels.

# Easy Super Fudge Brownies

**MAKES 12**

10oz (300g) dark chocolate
12 tbsp butter
⅔ cup sugar
2 tsp vanilla extract
4 eggs, beaten
1 cup all-purpose flour
2 tbsp cocoa powder
½ cup chopped walnuts
 or pecan nuts
vanilla ice cream to serve

**ESSENTIAL EQUIPMENT**
*13 x 9 x 2in (34 x 24 x 5cm)*
*baking tray*

• Line the baking tray with foil, letting it come up above the sides of the tray by about 2in (5cm).
• Preheat the oven to 300°F (150°C).
• Place the chocolate and butter in a heavy pan over a low heat. Stir constantly until smooth and glossy. Remove from the heat and leave to cool until tepid. Whisk the sugar, vanilla and eggs into the chocolate mixture until well blended. Stir in the flour, cocoa and walnuts or pecans until just combined.
• Pour into the lined tray and bake until the top is firm to the touch but the interior is still slightly gooey, 45 minutes. Place on a wire rack to cool completely. Use the foil to lift the brownie out of the tin. Cut into squares and carefully peel off the foil. Serve with a scoop of vanilla ice cream.

# Luscious Lemon Cheesecake

- Preheat the oven to 350°F (180°C).
- Combine the almonds, sugar, salt and butter. Press evenly on to the base of the pan. Bake until crisp, 10 minutes. Cool on a wire rack.
- Place the cream cheese in a bowl with the sugar, lemon zest and juice and beat briefly until smooth and creamy. Beat in the eggs a quarter at a time until just incorporated, scraping down the sides of the bowl after each addition.
- Spread the cheesecake mixture over the crust. Set the tin on a baking sheet and bake until the center jiggles slightly when the pan is tapped, about 45 minutes.
- For the topping, combine the sour cream, sugar and lemon juice. Spread over the baked cheesecake. Return to the oven and bake for another 5 minutes. Cool completely in the pan on a wire rack. Cover and chill in the refrigerator for at least 3 hours, preferably overnight.
- To unmold, run a knife around the sides of the cheesecake. Release the springform clip and remove the sides of the pan. Serve chilled, cut into slices.

**VARIATIONS**

## Luscious Lime Cheesecake

Omit lemon zest and juice and replace with the grated zest of 1½ limes and 2 tbsp lime juice for the filling, and 1 tbsp lime juice for the topping. Proceed as directed.

## Luscious Grapefruit Cheesecake

Omit lemon zest and juice and replace with the grated zest of ½ yellow grapefruit and 2 tbsp yellow grapefruit juice for the filling, and 1 tbsp yellow grapefruit juice for the topping. Proceed as directed.

---

**SERVES 6-8**

FOR THE CRUST
2 cups ground almonds
3 tbsp sugar
pinch salt
4 tbsp melted butter

FOR THE FILLING
2lb (1kg) cream cheese
1⅔ cups granulated sugar
grated zest of 1 lemon
2 tbsp lemon juice
4 eggs, beaten

FOR THE TOPPING
1 cup sour cream
4 tbsp sugar
1 tbsp lemon juice

**ESSENTIAL EQUIPMENT**
*1 x 10in (25cm) springform cake pan*

**HEALTH BITE**
Lemon peel contains more vitamin C than the flesh itself, but non-organic lemons are treated with waxes, fungicides and post-harvest sprays to prolong shelf-life and improve eye-appeal. These cannot be completely removed by washing. If you can't find organic lemons to zest, we advise leaving out the grated zest altogether.

# Chocolate **Truffle** Torte

**SERVES 6-8**
FOR THE CAKE
10 tbsp butter
14oz (400g) dark chocolate,
  broken into pieces
⅔ cup granulated sugar
5 eggs, separated

FOR THE GLAZE
¾ cup heavy cream
6oz (175g) dark chocolate,
  broken into pieces

ESSENTIAL EQUIPMENT
*1 x 10in (25cm) cake pan,
buttered and lined with baking
parchment*

**COOK'S TIP**
How do you tell when you have
whisked the egg whites to soft
peaks? Lift up some of the egg
white foam with the whisk – the
peaks will hold their shape but
droop slightly when the whisk is
lifted out.

• Preheat the oven to 300°F (150°C). Butter and line the cake pan.
• For the cake, place the butter and chocolate in a heavy saucepan over a low heat. Stir constantly until smooth and glossy. Remove from the heat and leave to cool until tepid. Whisk the sugar and egg yolks into the chocolate mixture.
• Place the egg whites in a large bowl and whisk until soft peaks form. Use a rubber spatula to fold a quarter of the egg whites gently into the chocolate mixture. Add this mixture to the remaining egg whites and gently fold together. Pour into the prepared cake pan. Bake until the top is firm to the touch but the interior is still slightly gooey, 45 minutes. Leave to cool completely on a wire rack.
• For the glaze, heat the cream in a small pan until just below simmering. Remove from the heat. Add the chocolate and leave to stand for 1 minute. Stir until smooth and glossy. Leave to cool until slightly thickened, 30 minutes.
• To unmold the cake, run a knife around the sides of the pan. Turn out and peel off the paper. Reinvert onto a serving dish. Spread the glaze over the cake. Serve in wedges, with garnishes if using.

CHOCOLATE TRUFFLE TORTE GARNISHES
You can serve this torte unadorned or dress it up with various simple garnishes. Choose from:

strawberries, halved, or raspberries to decorate, cream, whipped, thick or pouring, to serve, cocoa, to dust.

Or for an impressive final flourish, serve with a berry coulis. Purée a handful of fresh or frozen strawberries and/or raspberries in a blender until smooth. Drizzle this berry coulis around the wedges of torte just before serving.

# Spiced Apple Crumble Cake

- Preheat the oven to 375°F (190°C).
- For the crumble, place the flour, sugar and butter in a food processor; pulse until coarse and crumbly. Alternatively, mix the flour and sugar by hand and, using 2 knives, cut the butter into the flour mixture. Set aside.
- For the fruit, combine the apple slices with the sugar and cinnamon until evenly coated.
- For the cake, sift the flour and baking powder together and set aside. Beat the eggs together with the milk. In a large bowl, beat the butter until light and creamy. Gradually beat the sugar into the butter until white and fluffy. Gradually add the egg mixture, about 1 tbsp at a time, beating thoroughly after each addition. Use a rubber spatula to fold in the flour in 3 batches.
- Spread the cake mixture evenly into the prepared pan. Cover the cake mixture with the apples. Sprinkle the crumble over the apples. Bake until the crumble is golden brown, the apples are tender and the sides of the cake have pulled away from the pan, about 1 hour.
- Leave to cool on a wire rack for 15 minutes, then run a knife around the sides of the cake and turn out on to a serving dish. Serve warm or at room temperature.

**VARIATIONS**

## Rhubarb and Ginger Crumble Cake

Replace apples with 1½ lb (750g) rhubarb cut into ½ in (1cm) pieces. Replace cinnamon with ground ginger. Proceed as directed.

## Blackberry and Apple Crumble Cake

Reduce apples to 2 and add ½ quart (250g) blackberries. Proceed as directed.

## Cranberry and Orange Crumble Cake

Replace apples with ½ quart (250g) cranberries. Add the grated zest of 1 orange. Increase the sugar to 4 tbsp. Proceed as directed.

---

**SERVES 6-8**

FOR THE CRUMBLE
1 cup all-purpose flour
¼ cup granulated sugar
6 tbsp butter

FOR THE FRUIT
4 apples, sliced
1 tbsp sugar
1 tsp cinnamon

FOR THE CAKE
6oz (175g) all-purpose flour
2 tsp baking powder
3 eggs
1 tbsp milk
12 tbsp butter, softened
¾ cup granulated sugar

**ESSENTIAL EQUIPMENT**
*1 x 10in (25cm) cake pan, buttered and lined with baking parchment*

**COOK'S TIP**
The secret to successful cake-making is to have all the ingredients at room temperature. Here are 2 quick-fixes if you have forgotten to take the butter or eggs out of the refrigerator.
To soften butter, cut into small cubes. Place in a bowl set over another bowl of just boiled water, making sure the base of the bowl is not actually touching the water or the butter will melt, not soften. Set aside to soften, about 10 minutes. To bring eggs to room temperature, place whole eggs in their shells in a bowl of hand-hot water for 10 minutes.

# Mini Pavlovas with Summer Berries

**SERVES 8**

**FOR THE MERINGUE**
6 egg whites
1⅔ cup superfine sugar
2 tsp cornflour
1 tsp vinegar

**FOR THE TOPPING**
1 cup heavy cream
1lb (500g) strawberries, raspberries, blueberries or blackberries or a combination

**COOK'S TIP**
It is crucial that the bowl in which you beat the egg whites is completely grease-free or the egg whites will not stiffen. If in doubt, wipe with paper towel, dipping in vinegar before you begin. To achieve maximum volume, be sure that the egg whites are at room temperature before you beat them. A daring but effective way to check if the egg whites are sufficiently stiff is to hold the bowl upside down: the meringue should not fall out.

- Preheat the oven to 350°F (180°C).
- Line 2 baking sheets with baking parchment. Draw 4 x 4in (10cm) circles onto each parchment sheet.
- Place the egg whites in a large bowl and beat until soft peaks form. Gradually beat in the sugar, 1 tbsp at a time, beating well after each addition. Beat until the whites hold stiff peaks. Gently beat in the cornflour and vinegar.
- Divide the meringue mixture equally among the circles. Spread into rounds with a rubber spatula. Use the back of a spoon to hollow out a nest. Bake for 5 minutes. Turn down the oven to 250°F (120°C). Bake until crisp on the outside and gooey inside, 45 minutes. Place on a wire rack to cool completely before peeling off the parchment paper.
- Whip the cream until just stiff. Top the pavlovas with cream. Arrange the berries over the cream. Serve chilled or at room temperature.

**VARIATION**
## Mini Pavlovas with Banana and Chocolate
Omit summer berries and replace with 2 bananas, sliced and gently tossed in 2 tbsp lemon juice. Place 2½oz (75g) dark chocolate and 3 tbsp heavy cream in a small saucepan over a very low heat. Stir constantly until the chocolate has just melted. Remove from heat and stir until smooth and glossy. Leave to cool until slightly thickened, 5 minutes. Arrange bananas over cream. Drizzle over melted chocolate. Dust with cocoa powder to garnish.

# Breakfast Anytime

# Blue Moon
# Muesli Smoothie

Place the blueberries, dates, oats, almonds, banana, apple juice and soy milk in a blender; whizz until smooth.

**SERVES 1**
4 tbsp blueberries
2 dried stoned dates
2 tbsp rolled oats
5 almonds
1 small banana
½ cup fresh apple juice
⅓ cup vanilla soy milk

# Banana Bliss
# Smoothie

Place banana, soy milk, yogurt and honey in a blender; whizz until smooth.

**SERVES 1**
2 bananas
¾ cup vanilla soy milk
4 tbsp yogurt
1 tsp honey

**HEALTH BITE**
Potassium-rich and high in complex carbohydrates, bananas pack an energy giving nutritional punch that makes them a great way to start the day.

Easily digestible, soy milk is a great substitute for those wishing or needing to avoid dairy milks. Low calorie, low in cholesterol and low in carbohydrate, it is also an excellent source of vegetable protein. Choosing organic soy milk is imperative if you wish to avoid genetically modified soy products.

# Berry Breakfast Pancakes

**SERVES 4**

2 cups all-purpose flour
1 tbsp baking powder
½ tsp salt
2 eggs, beaten
1 tbsp sugar
2 cups milk
2 tbsp melted butter
8 tbsp blueberries or
  raspberries or a combination
oil to brush griddle or pan

FOR SERVING
maple syrup or honey

**ESSENTIAL EQUIPMENT**
*cast-iron griddle or large skillet*

• Preheat the oven to 350°F (180°C).
• Place the flour, baking powder and salt in a large bowl and make a well in the center. Add the eggs, sugar, milk and butter to the well. Gradually draw in flour from the sides and whisk to a smooth batter. Gently stir in the berries. Transfer the batter to a large glass measuring cup.
• Heat the griddle or pan over medium heat and brush with oil. Working in batches, pour enough batter to make 4in (10cm) pancakes onto the hot griddle or pan. Cook until bubbles appear on the surface and the underside is golden brown, 3 minutes. Turn pancake, pressing gently to ensure that the pancake is in contact with the griddle or pan. Cook until underside is brown, 2 minutes.
• Transfer the pancakes to a baking sheet and loosely cover with foil and keep warm in the oven while you cook the remaining pancakes. Brush the griddle or pan with oil between each batch of pancakes. Serve hot with maple syrup or honey.

**VARIATIONS**

## Rice Pancakes

Omit berries. Add 8 tbsp cooked brown or white rice to the batter. Proceed as directed.

## Raisin Pancakes

Omit berries. Add 8 tbsp raisins to the batter. Proceed as directed.

## Whole Wheat Pancakes

Omit berries. Replace all-purpose flour with whole wheat flour. Proceed as directed.

## Yogurt Pancakes

Omit berries. Reduce milk to 1 cup. Add 1 cup yogurt with the eggs, sugar, milk and butter to the flour. Proceed as directed.

## Banana Pancakes

Omit berries. Have ready 1 sliced banana. Make batter as described. Pour batter on the hot griddle or pan and immediately place 2 slices of banana on top of each pancake. Proceed as directed.

# New Orleans
# French Toast

**SERVES 4**

3 eggs, beaten
1 tbsp sugar
¼ tsp salt
1 tsp vanilla extract
½ cup heavy cream
½ cup milk
8 slices day old white bread
1 x 4oz (125g) stick butter

FOR SERVING
maple syrup or honey

- Preheat the oven to 350°F (180°C).
- Place the eggs, sugar, salt, vanilla, cream and milk in a large bowl. Beat until well blended and foaming. Dip the bread slices in the egg mixture, turning until well coated.
- Melt half the butter in a large non-stick skillet over medium heat. Add half the dipped bread and cook until the underside is golden brown, 3 minutes. Turn and brown the other side, 2 minutes.
- Transfer to a baking sheet and keep warm in the oven while you cook the remaining bread. Add the remaining butter to the pan as needed. Serve hot with maple syrup or honey.

# Mustard
# Scrambled Eggs

**SERVES 4**

2½ oz (75g) butter
8 eggs, beaten
6 tbsp grated gruyère or cheddar cheese
2 tsp dijon-style mustard
1 tbsp finely chopped fresh herbs (see opposite)
salt, black pepper

- Melt the butter in a saucepan over medium low heat. Add the eggs and cook, stirring constantly, until just thickened. Add the cheese and stir until melted. Remove from the heat. Stir in the mustard, herbs and salt and pepper to taste. Serve immediately.

**WHICH HERBS?**

Vary the fresh herb according to what is available. Our preference would be any one or a combination of parsley, chives, scallions, tarragon, watercress, sorrel or chervil.

**MAKES 12**

2 cups all-purpose flour
1 tbsp baking powder
½ tsp bicarbonate of soda
½ tsp salt
2 eggs, beaten
1 cup light brown sugar
1 cup yogurt
1 x 4oz (125g) stick butter,
   melted
1 tsp vanilla extract
1 cup blueberries
sugar and ground cinnamon
   for dusting

**ESSENTIAL EQUIPMENT**
*12-cup muffin tin, buttered or
lined with paper cups*

**COOK'S TIP**
You can bake muffins up to 1 day
in advance. Store in a sealed plastic
bag at room temperature.

# Best Blueberry Yogurt Muffins

• Preheat the oven to 375°F (190°C).
• Sift the flour, baking powder, bicarbonate of soda and salt into a large bowl. Place the eggs, sugar, yogurt, butter and vanilla in a second bowl and beat until blended. Add the egg mixture to the flour with the blueberries. Use a rubber spatula to fold together gently until just combined. Do not overmix; the mixture should not be smooth. Divide the mixture among the muffin cups. Sprinkle over a dusting of sugar and cinnamon.
• Bake until the edges shrink from the sides of the pan into the muffins comes out clean, 12-15 minutes.
• Leave the muffins in the pan for 5 minutes before removing. Run a knife around the edges of the muffins. Turn out onto a wire rack. Serve while still warm or at room temperature.

**VARIATIONS**
## Spiced Banana Yogurt Muffins
Replace the blueberries with 2 diced bananas and 2 tsp ground cinnamon. Proceed as directed.

## Cranberry Nut Yogurt muffins
Replace the blueberries with 1 cup cranberries and ½ cup chopped pecans or walnuts. Proceed as directed.

## Lemon Pear Yogurt Muffins
Replace blueberries with 2 diced pears and the grated zest of 1 lemon. Proceed as directed.

# Seasonal Menus

## A Perfect Day for a Picnic

*Good food always tastes better outdoors, whether on the beach, in the park, or at home on the lawn. Picnics call for dishes that travel well and this menu is perfectly portable. Everything can be made in advance. To ensure a crisp crust, let the pizzas cool completely on a wire rack before slicing and wrapping.*

Spinach, Blue Cheese and Pine
Nut Pizza (see page 49)
Marinated Beans with Lemon, Oil
and Chili (see page 101)
Roast Pepper, Artichoke and Feta
Salad with Arugula (see page 42)

•

baguette or crusty peasant loaf
assorted cheeses

•

ripe melon slices and bunches of
green grapes
Easy Super Fudge Brownies
(see page 120)

•

lemonade or limeade

## An Autumn Harvest Menu

*A richly colored vegetarian menu that celebrates the turning of the season, when late summer produce is still gloriously abundant and the first winter squashes make their appearance on the market stalls.*

Olive Oil Bruschetta with Red Pepper
and Almond Pesto (see page 54)

•

Ginger Squash Soup (see page 30)

•

Mushroom Tart (see page 65)
Balsamic Baked Onions (see page 110)
Slow-Roast Tomatoes (see page 100)

•

Upside Down Red Plum Caramel Cake
(see page 114)
crème fraîche

## Sunny Weekend Wake-up Breakfast

*Set the table outside on the terrace or by an open window. Then relax and read the papers in the morning sunshine.*

Blue Moon Muesli Smoothie
(see page 133)

•

Mustard Scrambled Eggs
(see page 137)

•

summer fruit bowl of peaches,
cherries and apricots

•

coffee, tea

## Self-Serve Dinner Party

*Gently bubbling pots of soups on the stove make cooking for a crowd easy. Your guests are greeted by the comforting aromas of steaming soup and warm bread. If you like to bake, turn to page 53 for our focaccia recipe and choose from simple olive oil, rosemary, olive and onion, or, better still, serve a selection.*

Tuscan Vegetable Soup with Greens
and Beans (see page 20)
Carrot and Parsnip Soup with Ginger
(see page 24)
Potato, Garlic and Fennel Soup
(see page 23)
baskets of assorted warm breads

•

Blueberry-Pear Crisp with Oatmeal
(see page 119)
vanilla ice cream

## A Mostly Moroccan Menu

*A feast of flavors to brighten any winter evening. Set your table to match: cover with a bright cloth and arrange the food on colorful platters.*

mixed cured olives
Moroccan Spiced Carrot Soup
(see page 24)
warm flat bread

•

Coriander Roast Lamb with Spiced
Chickpea Sauce (see page 71)
Roast Winter Roots (see page 102)
buttered couscous

•

chilled sliced oranges
a winter fruit plate of dried apricots,
dried figs and fresh dates

## An Intimate Fireside Supper

*As the evenings darken and the air turns cold, it's time to ward off the winter blues with this special menu. Candlelight, best china, white linen, and good friends essential.*

Watercress, Chicory and Smoked
Salmon Salad with Horseradish Dressing
(see page 38)

•

Pan-Roast Chicken with Herbed
Goat Cheese (see page 62)
Carrot Smashed Potatoes (see page 94)

•

Chocolate Truffle Torte (see page 124)

## Sunday Lunch at Home

*A just about all-year round menu that sticks to all the best Sunday lunch traditions, jazzed up with a few new ideas.*

Potato, Garlic and Leek Soup
(see page 23)

•

Perfect Roast Chicken with Green Olives
and Lemon Roast Potatoes (see page 77)
Sizzling Garlic Greens (see page 92)

•

vanilla ice cream
Chocolate Fudge Topping (see page 116)

## A Midsummer Feast for Friends

*Set the table in a shady spot in the backyard and open a chilled bottle of crisp white or rosé.*

Bruschetta with Avocado Goat Cheese
(see page 56)

•

Roast Red Pepper and Tomato Soup
with Basil (see page 26)

•

Grilled Eggplant Pizza with Basil
(see page 50)
a leafy salad of seasonal greens
Lemon Garlic Dressing (see page 108)

•

Luscious Lemon Cheesecake
(see page 123)
ripe strawberries

## A Sit-Down Family Brunch for a Winter Weekend

*Brunch is the most relaxed of meals and a good choice for a casual family get-together. All the dishes can be prepared well ahead of time and only need a few minutes in the oven to warm through. Mimosas - freshly squeezed orange juice and champagne - complete this classic menu.*

Onion Tart (see page 65)
a leafy salad of seasonal greens
Honey Mustard Dressing (see page 108)

•

Lemon Pear Yogurt Muffins
(see page 138)
Cranberry and Orange Crumble Cake
(see page 127)
a winter fruit bowl of mandarins,
bananas and kiwis

•

coffee, tea

## Easy Weekday Suppers

*If you fancy a proper sweet and sticky ending, look no further than our quick-fix toppings for vanilla ice cream - toffee banana, very berry, caramelized apple and chocolate fudge (see page 116).*

### Spring Supper
Spiced Green Lentil Soup with Spinach
and Lemon (see page 29)

•

yogurt with sliced banana and
a drizzle of honey

### Summer Supper
Red Peppers Stewed with Potatoes and
Olives (see page 92)

•

a fruit plate of sliced peaches and
strawberries

### Autumn Supper
Roast Cherry Tomato Spaghetti
(see page 69)

•

ripe pears, walnuts and a wedge of
blue cheese

### Winter Supper
Red Lentil Dhal with Aromatics
(see page 82)
steamed rice

•

mandarins

## Late Summer Grill Dinner

*Backyard barbecue parties are an easy way to entertain. While your guests gather round the grill, let the savory, smoky aromas set their appetites on fire!*

Bruschetta with Avocado Goat Cheese
(see page 56)

•

Grilled Vegetable Platter with Pesto
Dressing (see page 37)
Grilled Balsamic Lamb Chops
(see page 82)
New Potato Salad with Shallot
Vinaigrette (see page 111)

•

Mini Pavlovas with Summer Berries
(see page 128)

## French Farmhouse Feast

*Festive fare with a French accent for family and friends. Accompany with a full-bodied red wine and have plenty of bread at hand.*

Potato, Garlic and Parsley Soup
(see page 23)

•

French Leek Tart (see page 65)

•

Slow-Simmered Beef Daube with Red
Wine and Garlic (see page 78)

•

country-style bread
French cheese platter

•

Upside Down Apple Caramel Cake
(see page 114)
crème fraîche

## It's Springtime!

*Celebrate spring with this light lunch menu that pays homage to the fresh produce of the new season. Rather than using mixed vegetables for the platter, grill tender asparagus spears and choose parsley rather than basil for making the pesto dressing.*

Grilled Vegetable Platter with Pesto
Dressing (see pge 37)

•

Spring Vegetable Ragoût (see page 104)
warm crusty bread

•

Strawberry-Rhubarb Crisp with
Oatmeal (see page 119)
vanilla ice cream

# Index

# Index

EDITORIAL CONSULTANT
Rosie Kindersley
DESIGN AND ART DIRECTION
Stuart Jackman
PROJECT EDITOR
Sally Somers
PRODUCTION MANAGER
Maryann Webster

FOOD STYLING
Eric Treuillé

## Acknowledgments

Eric Treuillé would like to thank:
As ever, my wife Rosie, for
making it all happen, again.
Julia Pemberton Hellums, for
making sense of it all, again.
The Books for Cooks Team,
especially Victoria Blashford Snell
and Ursula Ferrigno, for their
passion for good food and their
willingness to share their
inspiration with us.
Sally Somers, for the dhal lesson
and for arguing about everything -
both much appreciated.
Ian O'Leary, for fabulous photos,
of course, but also for giving me
the chance to work with a
photographer, rather than just
for one.
Stuart Jackman, for giving us the
opportunity, for being on board,
for making this one so damn
gorgeous.

Renée Elliott would like to thank:
Brian, my husband, for his
unconditional support. My mom,
for celebrating food and cooking.
My dad, for the vegetable garden.
Rosie Kindersley, for bringing it
all together. And Peter, her father,
for making this possible.